How To Be A Goalie Parent

Brian Daccord

How To Be A Goalie Parent

Acknowledgments

For the past twenty-five years, I have had the opportunity to work with motivated goalies from virtually around the world. This would not have been possible without their parents trusting me to treat their children with respect and to give them everything I could as a coach and mentor. I can't thank those parents enough for believing in my teaching system as well as in me, as a person.

Whenever I advise goalies and goalies' parents, I always ask myself the same question: "what would I say if the goalie we were discussing was my son or daughter?" Hopefully, this methodology has led to frank and honest advice that is free of bias or any agendas. I have brought the same mindset in *"How to Be a Goalie Parent."* I hope this book gives real answers to real questions and helps goalies and their parents along their journey.

It truly takes a village to build a goalie and it's no different in putting this book together. My wife, Daniela, worked tirelessly to proof each page, and considering they call me the "Typo King" around the office, you can imagine the effort it took. My two sons, Joey and Alex, collaborated on the foreword and I am so proud of both of them. I can't say enough to the parents of the professional goalies who sacrificed their time to give back and help other goalie parents. My wonderful journey in the world of goaltending started with a father who created opportunities for me, a mother who sacrificed her time and doubled as a hockey bus driver, and a stepmom whose positivity inspired me to believe in myself. I am grateful for the opportunity to write this book and appreciate your dedication to your goalies.

Dedication

"To all goalie parents, whose sacrifice and support allow their children to play the greatest position in all of sports."

Foreword

The first coach we ever saw at work was our Dad, Brian Daccord. From there, he has remained our best mentor, yet most importantly, he has been the best Dad that we could have ever asked for. We both began playing goalie as little kids and worked our way up through youth hockey, prep school, and college. Even I, Joey, have played in the NHL.

I still hear the stories of the first time that my parents, Brian and Daniela, brought me to the hockey rink when I was only one week old. Little did I know that I was going to have unlimited access inside one of the best goaltending minds that hockey has ever had to offer. We have always been a hockey family through and through, and that was because of my Dad. I started with one-on-one lessons at 6 years old with my dad for 16 weeks before I ever played for an organized team, and I can remember my nickname was "Joey the Pro" because of how well trained I was. My Dad guided me, coached me, and mentored me from the first time he taught me how to skate, all the way to the time I came off the ice after my first NHL game where we shared a very special moment together, and beyond.

All of the hockey moments, the successes, the failures, the time around the rink we have shared together, have been some of the best parts of my hockey journey. But to be quite honest, none of that compares to our relationship and the way he has guided me off the ice. I would not be the man I am today without his direction. He always put my brother, Alex, and me above himself, he always wanted what was best for us.

As the younger brother to Joey, I remember often looking up to both him and my Dad growing up in the game of hockey. I still remember going to rinks with Dad when I was younger, knowing that I was going to meet half of the individuals watching the game. The respect that they had for him always proved palpable. Through the years of goaltending, my parents ventured to strike the balance of seriousness and fun. They poured their hearts out into making our dreams come true. Eventually, through a multitude of adversity they did.

I will never forget my Dad sitting in the stands with Mom around his shoulder at my first college game, nor will I forget the text I received from Dad after. All that he has done for me in hockey pales in comparison to the job he has done for Joey and me as our Father. I cannot thank him enough for the man he has been, and the family he has crafted. I hope that the reader can see that the man writing the book has truly lived what he is venturing to share with you now.

There is no one more qualified to write this book than our Dad. He has worked in every possible role that a hockey coach can work, as an NHL goalie coach, an NHL goaltending scout, and NHL Director of Goaltending Operations and in the Front Office, as a youth hockey coach, a prep school coach, a junior coach, and a college coach. He has seen everything, met everyone, and achieved all there is to achieve in the hockey world over the 25+ years of coaching.

He has helped thousands of people through their journey in hockey, such as finding a new team in the middle of the season, helping a goalie get into a prep school or college, or just organizing ice time for a goalie to get the ice that they needed. He never refuses a call from a parent, and remains as genuine as when he was first trying to build his client base as a new goalie coach.

Everything you are about to read in this book, we have heard over and over again since we were first learning to skate. He has truly put his life's work into the development of the goaltending position, and has lived a second life through us. We hope that you can learn from his example.

Joey and Alex Daccord

Table of Contents

Introduction

Most everyone around the game of hockey has heard the adage:

"You must be crazy to be a goalie."

But not as many are familiar with the extension that follows:

"You must be even crazier to be a goalie parent."

Once you dive into the world of goaltending you eventually find out that neither is true. Being a goalie parent is a ride like no other, filled with highs and lows and the thrill of watching your son or daughter play a position and sport that fills them with joy, passion, and the need to meet and exceed expectations. As for the goalies themselves, there is no quote that better sums up the position than that of the legendary Vladislav Tretiak:

*"There is no **position** in **sport** as **noble** as goaltending."*

When asked what I and my wife Daniela do for a living, our answer isn't the one that you would expect. I could answer that I have been in professional goaltending development for the past 25 years since retiring as a goalie myself, having the opportunity to be the goalie coach for the Boston Bruins, a goaltending scout for the Toronto Maple Leafs, director of goaltending operations for the Arizona Coyotes and my most recent position as goaltending coach of the Boston University Terriers. Daniela could reply that her full-time job is as an academic supervisor of "The Bridge ", a progressive program for motivated elite goalies that combines academic and athletic goals, but that wouldn't be much fun. Our answer to what we do for a living is always tongue in cheek:

How To Be A Goalie Parent

"We breed goaltenders!"

We are proud parents of two goaltenders and have supported them through their trials and tribulations in between the pipes. Our older son, Joey Daccord, is a former member of the Ottawa Senators and is now with the new expansion team the Seattle Kraken, and our younger son, Alex Daccord, is a goaltender for St Anselm College located in Manchester, New Hampshire. We are also tremendously fortunate to have played a role in the journey of hundreds of goalies that have trained at *"Stop It Goaltending,"* our goaltending development company based out of Massachusetts. Having the opportunity to be a part of the success of so many goaltenders, we wanted to share that knowledge with other parents looking to do whatever they can to support their goalies.

In our home, raising two goalies was a team effort and it is no different in writing this book. My role was to take all the experience I have had as a former professional goalie, a dad, goalie coach, and scout and condense 25 years of experience into a format that would help goalie parents apply that knowledge for their goalies. Daniela's role was to help with proofing this book and make sure that I properly provided practical knowledge to all goalie parents including ones like her who may have had little or no knowledge of hockey before their kids, for whatever reason, decided to be goalies. We hope you enjoy the guidance and stories contained in this book and the advice of the goalie parents of current NHL goalies and accomplished female goalies on their kids' journey and the factors that played a role in their success.

Preface

I began writing this book shortly after my older son, Joey, played his first game in the NHL. It was the events of this game that inspired me to put my experiences as a goaltending coach, scout, mentor, and parent into a book that could help other goaltenders. Joey's team — Arizona State University — had been eliminated from the NCAA regional championships five days earlier and after joining the Ottawa Senators shortly thereafter, he was awarded his first start. It happened to be in a sold-out KeyBank Center in Buffalo on Jack Eichel bobblehead night and was the Sabres' last home game of the season. Ottawa was sitting in last place and playing their third game in four nights. If I am being totally honest, I was more nervous for that game than I had been for both my sons' births.

My wife, Daniela, our younger son, Alex, Joey's two best friends, and a previous next-door neighbor, who was also a goalie Dad, hopped on a flight to Buffalo the morning of the game. This was the start of 24 hours of recalling stories and memories of the journey that preceded this magical moment. A few hours before the game, I settled in the hotel next to the rink for a nap only to find it impossible to sleep so I decided to get up and go for a run. Shortly after, I was on my way running along the canal, breathing heavily and with a good sweat on, when it dawned on me that I was not a runner and I had no idea why all of a sudden I needed to run!

An hour before the game, our group met up in the hotel lobby with my parents from Montreal, my sister's family from Toronto, and Joey's college hockey coaches as well as a booster from ASU. We made the short walk to the arena, a walk I knew all too well because Buffalo always hosts the NHL combine at the KeyBank Center and each team would conduct their prospects' interviews in the suites above the rink. Unexpectedly, after proceeding through security and entering the rink, my mother had a panic attack. In true French-Canadian fashion, the emotions of having her grandson play in his first NHL game hit her all at once. Being as nervous as I was, I think this helped me because I could focus on her and make sure that she was going to be ok. We made our way to a suite I had rented for our group. This will be my first piece of advice: If you do get to go see your son play his first NHL game and can be joined by family and friends, rent a suite. The experience of sharing this special moment with people who all played a role in him getting to this point was priceless.

I vividly remember the words of Joey's college coach, Greg Powers, before the opening puck drop. Greg is a former college goalie himself and a respected Division I NCAA hockey coach. Coach Powers looked at me before the game started and said, "I never knew what it meant to be a goalie parent until tonight. I don't think I have ever been this nervous before a game." After the first period, the Senators had a slim 2 to 1 lead and once again he uttered a gem. I can't believe how long that first period took, it felt like watching the entire length of a game. It was so striking to me that a former goalie and current college coach would experience the game like this.

In striking contrast to Coach Powers and me, my wife was all smiles and was having the time of her life. The suite paid huge dividends for me as I was able to move around and walk the concourse in between periods. The Sabres ended up putting 40 shots on net and won 5 to 2. Joey battled hard, made some big saves, and watching him walk up the stairs to the family waiting area and hugging his mother is a moment that's etched in stone for me. Joey and I both shed a tear and we embraced. We both uttered the words as if scripted, "we did it!"

What hit me during those 24 hours was how much was involved in getting to that point. All the decisions that had to be made like whether to be a goalie or a player, where to play, whether to leave home and where to go to school. The list goes on and on. By no means is this a book solely for the parents of goaltenders whose kids want to play in the NHL or the Olympics. But what struck me was that if it was that hard for me, a former goalie who had a life that was immersed in the world of goaltending, how hard must it be for a parent without the same hockey resources. The goal of this book is to give goalie parents the best advice possible so they can give their kids the greatest enjoyment of the sport and the position and give back to the future parents of goaltenders that are going to face similar challenges as Daniela and I do.

My Hockey Background

I can't believe how fortunate I am to live my entire life as a goalie, goalie coach, goalie scout, goalie director and goalie dad. My journey started the day my older brother decided to quit being a goalie which left a set of pads in our house as fair game. Despite growing up in Montreal, I was a huge Bruins fan, especially Gerry Cheevers', the goalie of the Boston Bruins. Gerry is famous for his mask covered with stitches from where he got hit in the face with pucks. I thought that was the coolest thing ever and I wanted to be like him. Not only did he have cool equipment but he was also dynamic and exciting to watch. Needless to say, my father was not happy about my decision. At that time, I was a forward and had a knack for scoring goals. My brother quit being a goalie primarily because we played outdoors and he would freeze his butt off while playing. All in all, they both ended up the winners in the deal because now they had me to shoot on while we played on the backyard rink. I can still remember my dad with the snow blower clearing the rink for us to play and all the hours we spent having the time of our lives in our backyard.

Growing up on the West Island of Montreal, I played for our city's select team and then for Loyola High School. Other than my father, I didn't have a goalie coach and although he was a former center for the Montreal Junior Canadiens, he decided to learn as much as he could about the position so he could help me out. Back then, we didn't have access to goalie coaches like we have now or even the internet where we could watch videos about goaltending techniques and strategies. The way you learned to play back in the day was watching Hockey Night in Canada and copying the moves of your favorite goalie. From Loyola High School, I went on to the West Island Royals Junior "A" team and while I was with the Royals, I was recruited to play college hockey in the United States. I originally signed a letter of intent to attend the University of Maine but ended up at Merrimack College, a small school just outside of Boston, Massachusetts.

While at Merrimack College, I had a goalie coach by the name of Jim Logue. Jim was an All-American at Boston College, US Olympian, and tremendously knowledgeable about the position. Unfortunately, at that time, goalie coaching was not viewed as it is today and they could only bring Jim in sporadically. Playing college hockey in the NCAA was a tremendous experience and it allowed me to develop both on the ice and in the classroom. After three years at Merrimack College, I signed my first pro contract with Ambri Piotta in the Swiss National Hockey League where I spent the next six years. It was only at the end of my time in Ambri when they provided a part-time goalie coach. It was former Boston Bruin Marco Baron, and he was able to teach me some strategies that had an immediate impact on my game. My seventh season in Switzerland was the best and worst of times. I seriously injured my knee but also found the woman I would spend the rest of my life with.

My coaching career began at Merrimack College where I served as the goalie coach, an assistant coach, and the head coach of the junior varsity team. Transitioning from being a player to a coach was a lot more difficult than I thought. I learned from the Warriors' Head Coach, Ron Anderson, that being organized and prepared was the key to coaching and that understanding every aspect and every detail of the game helped develop a plan to prepare the goalies and the players for success. My next position was as a goalie coach at St. Anselm College in Manchester, New Hampshire. This was also the time I started in the hockey business developing what is now called *Stop It Goaltending*. Following an ECAC championship season at St. Anselm College, I was fortunate to be in the right place at the right time and be named the goaltending coach of the Boston Bruins in the NHL. While with Boston, my responsibilities also included the goalies in the American Hockey League. This was such a great learning experience for me and it allowed me to improve as a coach and to truly understand what it takes to get to the highest level of hockey.

Following my time with the Bruins, I coached prep school hockey as well as several independent organizations along with growing *Stop It Goaltending*. It was during that time, I served as goaltending coach for Adler Mannheim in the German DEL. After six seasons and one championship, I left Adler Mannheim and accepted a position as goaltending scout for the Toronto Maple Leafs in the NHL where I worked for five seasons. Transitioning from coaching to scouting was a great challenge and I am incredibly thankful for that opportunity. Scouting for the Leafs helped set up my next position as the Special Assistant to the General Manager and Director of Goaltending Operations for the Arizona Coyotes.

Not having a dedicated goalie coach throughout my entire career inspired me to become one myself. I thought I could give back and provide other goalies what I may not have necessarily received as a player. It wasn't that I didn't have good goalie coaches, it was just that the frequency of all of them working with me was not enough to get the results that could have made a big difference in my game. I am very proud to be part of a generation of coaching that provides goalies the specific training they need and an environment that is welcoming & nurturing while challenging all at the same time. Goaltenders and goal scorers are consistently engaged in a cat and mouse game with each side trying to get the upper hand. We must continue to think outside the box and find new and progressive ways to keep pucks out of the net.

Currently, I am the goalie coach at Boston University and with the help of the fantastic Stop It team, our company has grown to train over a thousand goalies annually across the State of Massachusetts. In writing this book, I drew on all the experiences that I've had as a coach, scout, director, and owner of a hockey goalie development business. Hopefully, I can give other goalie parents a look inside and share my knowledge and experience so they can do what they all want to do and that is to provide for their kids.

Daniela and I are the proud parents of two goalies ourselves. Both of them have had their own positive experiences and challenges, and it is through them that helped give me the perspective of not only as a goalie coach but as a goalie parent as well. My oldest son, Joey, a former member of the Ottawa Senators in the NHL and now he is with the Seattle Kraken and my younger son is entering his senior year at Saint Anselm College. Throughout this book, I will add some stories about my own experiences with my kids that might help add perspective to parents in similar situations. When I speak about goaltenders, I always say the same thing: I have tremendous respect for all the goalies who put on the pads and put themselves in the line of fire demonstrating courage and confidence in each and every game.

Ground Rules

Before we go any further in this book, there are a few ground rules to be discussed. These are some key things that if you learn early on in your journey as a goalie parent, may help you down the trail. Now, to be clear, every goalie's path is going to be different but there are always some underlying truths that come up constantly. Hopefully, this section will give you some golden nuggets of information that can help you and your son or daughter chart a path.

Don't Listen

As parents, we can all remember the day that our kids told us they wanted to be goalies. The question is why did they want to become goalies in the first place? What drew them to that position? A lot of times, you hear goalies explain that they love the position because they get to be a difference-maker, when the game's on the line, they can be the difference between winning and losing. Some goalies will tell you that they chose the position because they get to play the whole game. There is no doubt that the position is flat-out fun. To be in your crease and stare down the competition is a challenge. Athleticism, reactions, desperation, competition, all play into the drive to be between the pipes. When trying to find a way to explain to people why we choose to be goalies, I found this analogy to explain it best.

Often, I try to explain to people why someone would want to play goalie by using a baseball analogy that sums up exactly the thrill of playing between the pipes. Picture yourself watching a baseball game and the pitcher throwing a ball 100 miles per hour at a batter. The batter leans into the pitch and the ball explodes off the bat heading towards center field. The center fielder starts his dash as the ball is heading for the fence. Just as the center fielder gets to the fence he leaps in the air as high as he can and stabs at the ball. If he catches the ball, there is no home run and it is an unbelievable play. If he misses the ball the other team scores a run. There is such a thrill when the baseball player makes the catch that prevents a run and the crowd goes crazy on the play. Well, the thrill a baseball player gets catching a ball as he heads over the fence is the same thrill a goalie gets every time they stop a puck. The cool thing about playing goalie is you get to do it 20 to 40 times a game! Hopefully, now you can understand a little better why playing goalie is so much fun. But what about the pressure?

What about the fact that every time the goalie steps in the net they put themselves under the microscope. If a goalie doesn't play well the team often doesn't have a chance to win and all the players rely on the goalie putting their best foot forward. Therefore, it is clear that the goalie has the most pressure on them from the entire team, right? As a goalie coach for the Boston Bruins, I disagreed with the then-Head Coach, Robbie Ftorek. Robbie is one of the smartest people in hockey that I've ever met and has an interesting development story of his own. Robbie started as a figure skater and then transitioned into hockey. That time when he was honing his skating skills proved to be a difference-maker for him and one of the key reasons he made it to the NHL as a player. Robbie was an innovator and loved to think outside the box and challenge the norm.

But in this situation, I knew there was no way I was going to lose this argument because no one could convince me that the goalie didn't have the most pressure on him on the team. I guess I was wrong.

I can see his face as I tell this story, looking at me as he questioned me on who had the most pressure on the team. My answer was easy, it was the goalie. He asked me why wouldn't it be the second-line center, the sixth defenseman, or even the equipment manager? Why would it have to be the goalie? Maybe the second-line center is struggling with face-offs and feels that he is letting the team down, or maybe he hasn't scored in a month and is embarrassed, or maybe the coaches are all over him because of his defensive play. Maybe that sixth defenseman is scared that if he has one more bad game he's going to be sent back to the minors. What about the equipment manager? How do you know what's going on in the head of the equipment manager? That equipment manager can put more pressure on himself to do a good job than any of the players. Robbie explained that pressure is self-induced and that it comes down to the individual and how much pressure they put on themselves.

But the goalie position warrants being in a situation with imminent pressure, I continued to argue. Robbie countered this argument with the job of a brain surgeon. When a brain surgeon operates, one mistake and he or she could lose his or her patient. Now that's pressure, isn't it? But maybe that surgeon listens to AC/DC music in the operating room as they operate and during the operation holds a conversation with their fellow doctors and nurses about the latest movie that just came out. His point was that it all depends on the individual who puts pressure on themselves and the line that I will always remember is *"pressure is self-induced."* It all comes down to how goalies view their performance and can frame their performance. So it doesn't come down to the position, the coach, the fans, the agent, or even the parents. It all comes down to how the goalie views his or her role. It was at that time I started to understand that it was perspective that framed how you viewed everything as a goalie... and generally, as a person.

That being said you can't disagree with me on the fact that the requirements of the goalie are different from the players. I've been advising goalies and the families of goalies for over 20 years. And before we go any further, I'm going to tell you the same thing that I tell all the families that I consult. Do not listen to the other players' families. As far as I'm concerned, goalies play a different sport than forwards and defensemen. The requirements are different from the skills that they learn and the situations that they are faced with. The path of a goaltender does not mirror the path of a player. When it's time for decision making by goalie parents, they cannot look at them the same way as the decisions faced by other players such as what team to play for, how to communicate with a coach, skills training, off-season tournaments, choosing the right junior team, college or pro path. One of the biggest mistakes I see goalie parents make is following in the footsteps of players, sometimes even their own siblings.

There are so many decisions that have to be made for a goaltender. The expression that I use is that to maximize a goaltender's potential and reach the highest level that they are capable of, they must stay on the path. That path isn't the same for every goalie but they have to keep moving forward and be in a situation where they can improve. That may mean playing for a team that isn't in the top league or not playing for that team that is a perennial powerhouse and not seeing any shots. Staying on the path for a goalie is about being put in a situation where they can keep getting better. Improving every day is the key to making it in the long run and the better decisions that parents can make to keep their kids on the path may be the difference between achieving their goals or not. Therefore, when making decisions, I would highly recommend a goalie parent to consult someone that lives in the goalie world and can give them the advice that is needed and not the parent of a teammate who is a forward or defenseman. As we progress through this book, hopefully, I'll be able to give you some things to think about.

The Secret = games played → wiring of brain/body
seeing patterns

I know it's early in the book but we're going to get right into a secret that a lot of people don't understand and it took me a long time to figure it out. Moderation is key in life. You can't have too much or too little, you have to have balance. What is the balance for a goaltender? Balance for a goaltender is a combination of technique and athleticism. You don't want a goaltender who relies solely on his technical training but doesn't use his athleticism to make saves. You also don't want just an athlete who doesn't play the position technically. The issue with the goalies just being athletic and not trained is that they will not have consistency. But there is one special ingredient that is evident and I only really realized it when I was scouting and that is: *Games played.*

When I first took my scouting position for the Toronto Maple Leafs, I wanted to understand if there was any statistical information or an indicator that would help me choose which goalies to draft. In the NHL, as opposed to the NFL, the draft is primarily for 18-year-olds. Therefore, there is a lot of projection that goes into making a pick. So I studied the draft for the last 15 years to see if, statistically, there was anything that would increase the probability of a draft pick making it to the NHL. My thought was that if I could figure this out, it could increase my odds of making the right pick. Of course, as a scout, the odds aren't very good in drafting a goaltender. After my research, I found that I only had a 12.8% chance of picking a goaltender that would play at least a hundred games for the organization. In other words, if I picked one goalie every 8 years that would make it to the NHL, I would be average. That's not hard to figure out because usually about 21 goalies are being drafted each year. Of those 21 goalies typically only three become full-time goalies in the NHL. Now, of course, if I was only able to pick one NHL goaltender every 8 years, I'd probably be out of a job pretty quickly.

When I started looking at the numbers, I was pretty sure that save-percentage was going to be the stat that helped predict success. So, I first looked at save-percentage and goals-against average and there was no correlation between goalies that had good numbers and whether they were going to make it. Well, if the stat that was going to help me wasn't save percentage or goals-against average then it had to be the wins. But there was no statistical proof that a winning goaltender was more apt to make it as a draft pick.

Just when I thought there weren't any stats that would help me predict future success, all of a sudden the stat of games played (GP) jumped off the page. It was clear to me that the goalies who have played a lot of games had a better chance of being draft picks and having success in the NHL. The clearest example of this is goalies who play Major Junior Hockey in the Canadian Hockey League (CHL). The great thing about studying goalies in the CHL is that the record-keeping is done at a very high level. Therefore, you can trust the stats more than some other leagues. If you take a close look at those who played Major Junior Hockey there is a clear correlation between how many CHL games they played before the day they got drafted and their performance in the NHL.

In Major Junior Hockey, the age group is 16 to 20 years old and teams typically have an older goalie as their starter. That means the goaltender is usually 19 or 20 years old and the backup is traditionally a younger goaltender with the potential of being the starter. Most of the time, the goalies you need to evaluate are the backups when you are scouting Major Junior goalies. There are exceptions like when you have a talented younger goaltender, AKA

Carey Price or Marc-Andre Fleury, who both started for their junior team as 16/17-year-olds. By being a starter at a young age they inevitably had more games played than the other younger goalies in their draft year. So if you ever have a few hours on your hands and want to check NHL goalies that played Major Junior Hockey and how many games they played before the draft, you will see that the correlation to success is undeniable.

That correlation leads to the next question: Why are Games Played so important? The obvious answer is going to be: Experience. A goaltender with experience is going to be better than a goaltender that lacks experience. But what does that mean? Being a successful goaltender has a lot to do with pattern recognition. In a hockey game, you'll see the same patterns over and over again and a goalie with experience will be able to recognize those patterns and therefore anticipate what's going to happen, when it's going to happen and how it's going to happen. Not only does a goalie recognize the patterns of the plays they also see the release of a shot. Reading the release of a shot tells the goaltender where the puck is heading. The combination of reading the play and reading the release of the shot is essential for success and games played to allow the most opportunities to do this. Therefore, if you look at Carey Price of the Montreal Canadiens, he played as a starter early in the CHL and in the NHL. He has a ton of Games Played and therefore in goalie years, similar to dog years, when it comes to games played, Carey Price is currently probably in his sixties!

When you look at today's new breed of goaltenders no one stands out more than Carter Hart of the Philadelphia Flyers and Spencer Knight of the Florida Panthers. Carter Hart played major Junior Hockey in the WHL for Everett Silvertips where he played 109 CHL games before being drafted in the second round by the Flyers. At just 21 years of age, he became an NHL goaltender after only 18 games in the minors. Spencer Knight routinely

16

played 100 games a season in his peewee and bantam years. You will be able to read the interview from Spencer Knight's father Chris about how playing a lot of games and how they are balanced with other sports, training, school, and just being a kid later in this book.

In digging deeper into analyzing WHY games played are so important, you have to look at how the brain operates. Just remember I'm a hockey coach and not a neuroscientist but we'll break this down to its simplest level. A goalie does not have time to read a play and to read a release by simply thinking. Goaltenders think with their bodies, not with their brains. The easiest analogy to explain this is to think about driving a car. When you drive a car you are not thinking about how to hit the gas, or how to push the brake, or how often to check your rearview mirror, or even putting your blinker on when you're changing lanes. When you're driving a car, it is your body, not your brain, that's driving because you've done it so many times your body acts as the brain. A goaltender that has a lot of experience, AKA Games Played, focuses on the play and making the save and their body takes in all the cues that will help them predict what's going to happen in the play and on the shot release where the puck is going to go. Therefore every time a goalie faces a shot and watches the result of that shot they are building the tools necessary to have their body act like their brain.

If you ever want to watch videos about this concept of the body acting as the brain check out Dr. Joe Dispenza. Also, a great read on this theory is a book called "The Power of Habit" by Charles Duhigg. The crux of the book is a study that was conducted for people with short-term memory loss through either an injury or infection. These subjects could remember something that happened in high school but not something that happened yesterday. One of the subjects and his wife moved from their home to be closer to their daughter but still stayed in the study. Moving to a new home meant that the subject could not remember where any of the rooms in the house were or even simply how to turn on the television. He would routinely take walks in the neighborhood with his wife and always in the same pattern. Eventually, he started to take walks on his own and return to his house even though he had no memory of where the house was. What happened was his body learned, through the habit of walking the same path over and over, when to turn left and when to turn right. This was a breakthrough in the study and reading this book greatly impacted how I coached goalies from that point forward. I recognized that while training I would duplicate the same pattern over and over so the body could learn how to move while the mind focused on just stopping the puck.

Confidence

trying to make saves vs. trying not to get scored on

Before we go any further there is one thing you need to know about goaltending... Goaltending revolves around confidence. I've been in this business a long time and trained a lot of great goaltenders that were never able to translate their skills and talent onto the ice and perform at the same level that they train at. Having confidence trumps athletic ability, skill, and talent. If you think about sports, it is a microcosm of life, and playing goalie is no different. Without confidence it's hard to stop a puck in a hockey game and in life it's hard to land a job, make a sale, or get a date. If you look back on when a goalie plays well it is when he or she plays with confidence and plays in the moment.

So what exactly is confidence? Is it a feeling? Do you feel confident? I don't believe that confidence is a feeling... confidence for me is the ability to act. Think about it this way... what if you take control of your confidence? If confidence is merely a feeling, then it makes it more difficult to control. But if confidence is the ability to act, then you are in total control of your confidence. Therefore, let's take a look at how confidence applies to life. Showing confidence is walking into the interview for that job you want, confidence is making that phone call or knocking on that door trying to make a sale, confidence is walking up to the person you want to ask out on a date and asking the question. So these are all things that we can do to show confidence. While walking into that interview the feeling inside you may not be confident but the ability to walk into the interview is what is going to demonstrate the confidence you need. Walking up to that door and knocking, the feeling may not feel like confidence but knocking on that door is confidence. Getting ready to ask someone to go on a date may not feel comfortable but it is the confidence shown just by asking.

For a goalie, confidence is skating onto the ice and heading towards the net. As we move along in this book, we will talk about the importance for goalies to control what they can control and not get caught up in things out of their control. Skating on the ice and putting themselves on the line each and every game is a sign of confidence. As a scout, I want a goalie that has a presence on the ice and plays with confidence. It is one of the easiest things to spot. I look for a goalie who is in the net trying to make saves and trying to stop the puck which is a big contrast to the goalie that is in the net and trying not to get scored on. The goalie trying to make saves is acting and not just hoping the puck hits them. The goalie trying not to get scored on is hoping the puck hits them and it doesn't go in. It is something so easy for a scout to see and is a differentiating factor between one goalie and the next. So think about it this way, the goalie has shown confidence by getting in the net and then has to show confidence in acting while trying to stop the puck. In the act of trying to stop the puck, the goalie is demonstrating confidence and is now in control of their actions and not a passenger.

Improve through failure

A big component of a goalie's confidence is just his or her environment. The environment that has to be created is fueled by positivity and the recognition that the only way to improve is through failure. Positivity is non-negotiable and embracing failure is essential. Positivity will allow your goaltender to adopt a growth mindset and not inhibit them to take action. Creating a positive environment, where you choose your words carefully and teach, is the foundation of development. This does not mean that standards can't be high but it does mean that every time that there is a setback it is viewed as an opportunity.

So let's talk specifically about what that means for a goaltender and a goaltender's parents. When we're in the stands watching the game all we want is for our kids to have fun and hopefully be successful. Watching your son or daughter losing and letting in goals is not fun. We all have been there! But the truth of the matter is, those losses and the goals against will provide what's most necessary to improve and develop. There is a whole section in this book that includes advice on how to support and communicate with your goalie. If we go along the premise that confidence is the key to goaltending and that confidence is the ability to act, we as parents must create a positive environment where failure is accepted in order to provide them with what's necessary.

A Parent's Role

Now every parent has their own way of doing things and strategies on how to raise their kids. By no means am I going to suggest how to best parent your children but what I can provide is the insight of over 20 years of experience in the goaltending development field that might help you come up with a plan. Every child is different but there are certain approaches that I have found help goalies understand the position better and that will allow them to use their experiences to grow.

The very first thing every goalie should know is that playing goalie is what they do, not who they are. Being a good goalie is very important to the kids and they do drive a lot of their self-esteem from being a good goalie. Therefore, if things don't go well on the ice they take it personally, sometimes past the point of being healthy. If they derive their self-esteem primarily from what they do between the pipes they will end up being way too hard on themselves and lose some of the enjoyment of the game and life in general. Make sure your goalie knows that, more important than being a goaltender...they are a son, a daughter, a grandchild, a sibling, a friend, a teammate, and a leader... a person.

I have always been a big believer in the motto "dream big but don't expect big." Dreaming big and having high aspirations and goals are essential in their athletic development. If you're expecting those dreams to come true without accepting all the hard work and dedication required to make those dreams come true then you are mistaken. Typically 10% of all NHL goaltenders have trained, at some point, at Stop It Goaltending, my goaltending development company in Massachusetts. I have seen so many young goalies grow into Junior, College, and Pro athletes before my eyes. I have never been one to tell goalies that the chances of them making it to junior, obtaining a college scholarship, or playing in the NHL are very low. Could you imagine if I would have told Cory Schneider, when he was a freshman in high school, that there was a very small probability of him getting a scholarship to a college or playing in the NHL? I always say the same thing to the goalies and their parents... someone has to be the goalie for the Chicago Steel of the USHL, the London Knights of the OHL, Boston

University in Hockey East, and the Boston Bruins in the NHL. "Why can't it be you?"

To make it to one of these teams it's going to take a tremendous sacrifice and a whole lot of hard work. There will be plenty of highs and lows and the journey is not going to be an easy one. The only way to make it to the top and achieve young goalies' dreams is to be engaged at the level that they are currently playing. As the parent of a goalie playing in the pro's, it is incredible to have lived through the experience of watching him get there. I can't believe how long it takes to make it and that the real chore is to stick with the process and be committed and patient. I think where we as parents and goalies get off track is when they suffer adversity and try to find an easy way through it.

There is no fast way to get to the top. There is a great expression and it says the only way to the top is to take the stairs, not the elevator. There is no difference in the world of goaltending. Taking the stairs will give you all the lessons along the way and will give you the foundation to be successful at the highest levels. Too many goalies forget to "be where their feet are" and that means being present and engaged with the level they are playing at. Far too often the kids focus on what's next as opposed to what's now and their parents can feed into that. Goalies and parents need to stay fully engulfed in the team that they are with and not with their future team.

There is a simple rule that goalies have to figure out and the earlier they figure this out the better off they will be… play for the win. Goalies should be on the ice with their only objective to help the team win the game. As you read earlier about goalie stats, their statistics of save percentage and the goals-against average is not a predictor of success. So when out on the ice a goalie should be committed to doing anything they can to stop the puck. This applies to exhibition games, league games, playoffs, and tournaments. It especially applies when people are watching such as scouts and evaluators. A goalie's mistake is to play for his or her stats or play for scouts. The last thing a goalie wants to do is to be thinking about how they look or what people think about them as opposed to simply trying to help their teammates win a hockey game in any way they can.

Adversity

Often I see parents and goalies look to remove themselves from the situation where they are facing adversity to find another situation that may prove to be easier. When you hit the ages where the goalies are competing for ice time it may not be easy or even feel fair. But somehow, someway, goalies have to find their way and earn their time between the pipes. Being challenged and fighting for ice time and proving themselves is essential.

No matter how experienced and successful a goalie is, there will always be someone challenging him or her for their position. The easiest example to refer to is Martin Brodeur. Marty is arguably the greatest goalie that ever played the position. In 2013, The New Jersey Devils traded for goaltender Cory Schneider of the Vancouver Canucks and now, the great Martin Brodeur is 37 years old and has to prove himself all over again to get the net. In recent history, the Florida Panthers opted to use rookie goaltender Spencer Knight over Sergei Bobrovsky in back-to-back elimination games versus the Tampa Bay Lightning. Sergei Bobrovsky makes 10 million dollars a year and still has to prove himself. There are countless examples of goalies at every level throughout every season that have to compete for the net and prove to their teammates and coaches that they are the goalie for the team. Goalies should embrace the challenges and not run from them.

Goalie Parent Interview #1: Ken Swayman

1998 Anchorage-born and raised Jeremy Swayman is a goaltender for the Boston Bruins of the NHL. Swayman started out playing for the South Anchorage High School Wolverines before joining the Pikes Peak Miners 18U AAA program of the North American Hockey Prospects League. He made his way to the USHL where he played for the Sioux Falls Stampede and was selected in the fourth round of the 2017 NHL draft. At the University of Maine, he captured the 2020 Richter award his junior year as the top goaltender in the NCAA as well as the Hockey East Goaltender of the Year and Player of the Year award. Internationally Jeremy was a member of the 2017-2018 USA World Junior Championships team that won the Bronze medal.

When did your son decide to be a goalie?

Jeremy started skating actually very early at the age of two, and I went and got myself certified as a Level One coach just to be on the ice to help out. After he got through the learn to skate portion which included pushing the buckets called The Bucket Brigade he then graduated to the chair and you could tell he was one of the more polished kids on the ice. In kindergarten, Jeremy tried out for the Alaskan All-Stars and somehow he made the team despite the majority of the kids being two grades older than him. It was there where he started to thrive and loved every part of the goalie position and being around older kids helped speed his maturity.

What did you feel about that decision?

I wasn't involved in hockey but I grew up in NY and was a Rangers fan. I loved following the goalies and my brother would go to games and take pictures of the greats like Ed Giocomen and Gilles Villeneuve. Those pictures ended up on Jeremy's walls in his bedroom. I loved it and quite frankly just got a kick out of watching how much he engulfed himself in the culture of being a goaltender. I was also able to use his passion for hockey to convince him that school was just as important and he excelled in the classroom. We used to have season tickets to the University of Alaska Anchorage Seawolves division I college team and sat behind the net. Jeremy loved watching the goalies and would emulate them when we got home.

What has been the best part of the journey so far?

The best part of the goalie parent experience for me was way beyond hockey. Watching Jeremy blossom as a person was the best. He really got the message that it was about the team and not just him. Each year he learned lessons and matured and at each level had coaches and role models that he could learn from. The greatest thing is that I spent so much time trying to teach him and now I am learning from him. There is a lot of pressure that goes with being a goalie and I have learned a lot from Jeremy about how to be mindful and stay in the present. Nothing could be more gratifying for a parent than watching their son teach their father life lessons.

What has been the most challenging part of being a goalie parent?

The hardest thing for me as a goalie parent is the uncertainty of the uncontrollable. There is no way to control bad bounces and injuries and they can play such a big part of a game and a career. Not many people understand the sacrifices a goaltender must make to stay on top of everything. Nutrition, sleep, hydration... they all come into play. There is also the mental fatigue that goes with being a goaltender. Jeremy was lucky because he played with older kids and was the waterboy for the University of Anchorage Alaska. It was here that he went from sitting behind the net with me at games to watching how division one athletes prepare and handle themselves. Hockey players are the best and he would go talk to not only the Seawolves goaltenders but the visiting goalies as well. We must have 25 sticks from opposing DI goalies that came through town. Jeremy would talk to them after the games and end up with a signed broken stick more often than not.

What were the key aspects of his development that stand out to you?

I think this is really a blended question because becoming a successful goaltender is far beyond just skill development and being able to stop the puck. I know as a physician when I trained interns it was easy to tell which ones were going to be successful. They all gave 100% but the ones that went beyond 100% and gave 150% were the ones that stood out. The maturity a goaltender has to have both on and off the ice is what's going to help them in the long run. The goalie that just does what he has to do is going to have a hard time competing with the goalie who's trying to find different ways to get better not only as an athlete but as a person. When Jeremy attended a goalie camp when he was young the coach had worked with Eddie Belfour and told them a story about how, regardless of what Eddie was playing, he would not give up until he won. It didn't matter if it was darts or ping pong Eddie Belfour was extremely competitive and that was a big reason why he became a great goalie. When Jeremy was leaving for a game quite often there was a reminder to compete like Eddie Belfour.

Do you get nervous watching games and if so how do you combat those nerves?

I still get nervous at games but I am getting better and I'm using some of the strategies that I've learned from Jeremy to help me relax more and enjoy the game. I never like to be confined to one seat for the whole game as I prefer to move from end to end so you may find me in the walkway area if there are no seats available as opposed to being at the far end of the sheet.

One of the things that I really enjoy about being at the games is watching the little nuances and especially watching Jeremy interact with the kids in the crowd. I always reminded him that he was one of those little guys that loved watching the goalies and it meant so much to him when he was given a stick by a college goalie. I'm so proud of the way he interacts with his teammates and the fans and it makes me very proud as a father.

What is one piece of advice you would give other goalie parents?

We all know the analogy that you can lead a horse to water but you can't make them drink it. I think when it comes to goaltending it's important not only that we lead them to the ice rink but explain all the great life lessons that will come from being a hockey goaltender. One of those lessons is to be able to work with other people and be a great teammate. I think that Jeremy learned a lot from observing me as a surgeon and how important it was to be surrounded by a great team to have a successful outcome in the operating room. To be successful, the drive is going to have to come from them and there is no way a parent can dictate that or push. It is the goalie that will determine whether they have the passion and the drive to keep moving up through the ranks. As a parent, we can use the game of hockey to help our kids mature and grow as people regardless of what level they get to.

The Basics

All goalies must learn the basics and I'm not talking about the stance or any save technique. I'm talking about the core principles for all goaltenders. The earlier the goalies understand these principles the better off they're going to be. It is always a good thing to be reminded of the principals every once in a while to keep them on track. In this section, we'll go over each principal and how they apply. It may be a good idea to spend a little time with your goalie and discuss each one of the basic principles and review them from time to time.

1. Goalies must accept the two rules of goaltending. Rule number one is that you are going to get beat. Rule number two is you can't change rule number 1.

Accepting this rule is more challenging for some goalies than others. I don't think in the history of hockey there's ever been a goalie that has never given up a goal or lost a game, it is simply inevitable and part of the deal. We want goalies to be competitive and have a burning desire not to get scored on and to win but when it does happen goalies have to have the ability to let it go and move on to the next shot. In all my years in hockey and as a scout it has become evident to me accepting this inevitability is essential for success. As coaches, we talk about not looking through the rear-view mirror and keeping our eyes on the road ahead. Parents play a big role in talking to goalies through this and making sure that the goalies understand the rules of goaltending at an early age. There is always one-word used after a goal goes in or your team loses a game... and that is "Next."

"Next" i.e., goldfish

2. <u>Never get beat twice.</u> When goalies get scored on in practice be determined not to let the next shot in. This will train their mind so

that, if they get scored on in a game, they will quickly put it behind them and get ready for the next one.

There may never be a goalie in the NHL better than Martin Brodeur and despite all the games that he won including the Stanley Cups, his practice mantra may be the best piece of advice a former goaltender can give two younger goalies. When Martin Brodeur practiced he always used this mantra after he was scored on and that was... "Never get beat twice". After each goal in practice, by saying this mantra, he trained his mind to move past the point of being scored on and focus on making sure to stop the next puck. After each goal, he, therefore, had a heightened sense of urgency and focus. Often in practice, goalies get peppered with shots and it is extremely difficult to stay focused on all of them. What inevitably happens is that the goalie's focus level will start to drift. Using this mantra in practice trains the mind to immediately forget about the past, forget about the goal, put it out of your mind, and just concentrate on making the next save. Using this mantra in practice after practice, year after year, when a goalie gets scored on in a game, they now have the ability to move past the puck that just went in and prepare themselves for the next shot. This will lead to consistency and an overall higher level of performance.

3. Goalies need to pay the price. Stretch, sleep, watch their nutrition and stay hydrated as well as watching as much hockey on television as they can. They need to learn about technique, strategy, and equipment and prepare for practices and games as well as make the commitment away from the rink.

One of the lessons that parents consistently try to teach their kids is that nothing comes easy, they must earn what they get, and playing goalie is no different. Goalies need to pay the price if they want to be successful, it's not difficult to know what to do but actually doing it is the hard part. A goaltender has to do everything they can on and off the ice to create a differential between them and other goalies. One of the keys to having success is to stay on the ice and avoid injuries as best you can. Goalies need to stretch, watch their nutrition, stay hydrated and get their sleep. They need to be students of the game and watch hockey so they can learn from the best in the game. Goalies need to learn about technique and strategy and understand how to prepare for practices and games in order to maximize their time and improve consistently. Being a goalie isn't just something they do at the rink. Being a goalie is what they do on and off the ice after the rink and at home. There are so many things that a goalie can do at home such as conditioning, improving reflexes and now there is even virtual reality training that allows goaltenders to stop the puck in their own family room.

4. Have fun. The key to being successful at anything is to have passion when you are doing it. Goalies need to embrace the position and enjoy it every time they are on the ice. Coaches, parents, and teammates feed off their passion.

There is a reason why we say our kids "play" hockey and not "work" hockey. Hockey is meant to be fun and that's the reason we play it in the first place when hockey becomes work and something you have to do it will take the sheer enjoyment out of playing. Your typical goalie just absolutely loves being on the ice and playing the position. Parents need to fuel this passion because it is a passion that will get them through the hard times. Being a goalie comes with ups and downs and one of the keys to success is to not get too high and not get too low as a goalie. If a goalie is having fun playing the position and the sport they will be able to get through the lows because they have such a passion for playing. We need to fuel this passion with positive reinforcement, sound advice, and consistent support.

5. Goalies need to have a performance statement derived from what they do well when they are playing well and in the zone (ex. be aggressive and control the rebounds).

Being focused is essential for a goalie when they're playing but we all know that our inner self-talk can be our worst enemy. Having a performance statement is your primary way to challenge negative inner self-talk. Goalies can use their performance statement before they get on the ice, when they're squaring up for a face-off, or staring down an opponent on a breakaway. Constructing a performance statement is easy. A goalie simply thinks about what they do when they are playing well. In this example, we use "be aggressive and control my rebounds" and how the goalie uses this is to say it over and over again. By doing this it will drain out any negative self-talk that can happen. It is truly a magical technique and can make a dramatic impact in a goalie's game.

6. Goalies need to be an athlete first and a goalie second. It is essential to learn techniques and strategies but that cannot be the core of their game.

Being a goalie coach for over 20 years has allowed me to see the differences between why some goalies make it and some goalies don't. And one of those differences that continuously stands out in my mind is that the goalies that are truly athletes eventually outlast and outperform the goalies whose core is built on technique and strategy. Training technique and strategy should help the athlete and not hide the non-athlete. So as parents we have to make sure that our kids are playing different sports especially when they are younger. Both my kids played competitive soccer and tennis. My oldest son Joey was a captain of the hockey team, the soccer team, and the tennis team his senior year at prep school. I'm thoroughly convinced that playing these different sports and experiencing competition that required his body to do different things is a major factor to why he was able to make it to where he is now.

7. Control what you can control. There is so much that a goalie can't control so it is essential to take control of what you can.

Playing goalie is not like playing golf. When you play golf your score is based on your performance and you are in control of every shot. As a goalie, there are so many variables that can impact success or failure. A goal can result from a shot that hits a skate in front of the net and redirects in, a screen by either your own teammate or the other team and a goalie may be playing for a team that doesn't commit to defense or playing the right way. A goalie may even be better than his partner but for any number of reasons, the coach decides to play the other goaltender. These are all things that are out of a goalie's control and if they get caught up and worrying about things that they have no control over it will make it very difficult for them to do what they need to do.

8. Be accountable. No matter what happens do not point the finger at others and accept responsibility.

We just went over the fact that goals can happen for many different reasons, many of which are out of the control of the goalie. But the one thing that a goaltender cannot do is point the finger at other players for giving up a goal. Accepting responsibility is a trait that all goalies need to learn and in order to avoid issues, accept the responsibility and move on. It really doesn't help the goalie to make excuses and to point the finger at other reasons. There is usually something a goaltender could have done to help prevent a goal. Accepting responsibility will help build trust and respect between the goalie, their teammates, and coaches.

9. Goalies need to understand that they are simply a teammate just like everybody else on the team and should act accordingly.

Too often goalies ostracize themselves from the team because they act differently and do not incorporate themselves with the rest of the players. Take my advice, if a goalie wants to be successful they need to be liked and respected by the rest of the players. A goalie that blends in and is one of the group will lead to teammates making the extra effort to help the goalie by blocking shots, clearing any rebounds, and most importantly supporting the goalie when things don't go their way. The goalie that does not have strong relationships with their team and their coaches, and at the higher levels the equipment staff and trainers, will find that when things get rough they will not have the support that they need to get through it.

10. Goalies must learn the basic economic principle of supply and demand. There is only one net but more than one goalie. As they get older there is less demand and more supply. If they don't train for real now they won't be playing later.

The hard thing about being a goaltender is there is only one net and therefore only one goalie can play at a time. This does not apply to forwards and defensemen as typically, in a youth hockey game, there are nine forwards and six defensemen and at the higher levels twelve forwards and six defensemen. Therefore, if you're the second-best forward on a team you may still be playing on the first line, if you're the second-best centerman you may not be on the first line but you're probably centering the second line. You may not be the best defenseman on the team and therefore not on the first or second unit and playing special teams but you will get your shifts on the ice as part of the third unit. If you're the second-best goalie you may not get to play. As the kids move from equal ice time teams into play to win situations they must understand this principle.

1. you'll get beat
2. don't get beat twice
3. pay the price
4. have fun
5. performance statement → "be aggressive and control my rebounds"
6. athlete then goalie
7. control what you can control
8. be accountable
9. be a teammate
10. supply + demand

Goalie Parent Interview #2: Brenton Demko

Thatcher Demko is a 1995 born goalie who is currently playing goal for the Vancouver Canucks of the National Hockey League where he was a second-round draft pick in 2014. He began playing goalie in San Diego and then moved to the Junior Gulls. His early success led him to the Omaha Lancers of the USHL and then onto the U.S. National Development Team. He twice led the Boston College Eagles to the NCAA Frozen four and won the Mike Richter Award as the NCAA's most outstanding goalie in 2016. Thatcher has represented USA Hockey at the World Junior Championships two times, won a silver medal at the U-18 World Championships, and played for team USA at the Men's World Championships.

When did your son decide to be a goalie?

Thatcher started his interest in being a goalie when he was a Mite. The coaching staff on his team would rotate who played goalie each week to give each kid on the team an opportunity to try it. Thatcher volunteered every week. He would step up asking about it when he knew the player whose week it was didn't want to play! As part of the coaching staff on that team, I supported the head coach and continued the rotation but it was clear Thatcher was going to be a goalie.

What did you feel about that decision?

When Thatcher started playing travel hockey and made the team as a goalie, I fully supported him. I also made sure he continued to "play out" on his house league team, not wanting him to specialize in a position at such a young age. He did this through Peewees. He also played several other sports...soccer, basketball, baseball, lacrosse and participated in those other sports until he reached Bantams and decided to focus on hockey full time. Playing the other sports helped him develop as an athlete.

What has been the best part of the journey so far?

This is a tough question to narrow down to one specific part. Watching Thatcher pursue his passion and being able to support him in that journey has been tremendously rewarding for me. Watching Thatcher mature as a young man, how he handled the trials and tribulations of his journey has been remarkable. The people we have met, the relationships we have created are priceless. Thatcher has also had the opportunity to play around the globe so the travel has been pretty fun too.

What has been the most challenging part of being a goalie parent?

Finding consistent goalie coaching in southern California was challenging. There was a coach here locally that was very good for Thatcher when he was younger, but he was not consistently available. We had to learn on the fly. I studied the position enough to get by for those times where we had difficulty finding time with a goalie coach. There were a lot of trips up to Orange County & LA for lessons. In the off-season, we had to travel quite a bit for goalie camps as they were limited. Thatcher did not have a consistent goalie coach until he was playing U18 with the USA Hockey NTDP and we are grateful to the coaches he did have along the way.

What were the key aspects of his development that stand out to you?

Work ethic stands out the most. He is driven to be the best and listens to his coaches. He paid attention to the seminars that discussed the importance of being coachable, learning, etc. He also kept a goalie notebook, keeping notes on practices, games, etc. He truly became a student of the game, wanting to understand the nuances of the position and how to get better. His perseverance with the disappointment of getting cut, not getting drafted

(WHL, NAHL, USHL), his double hip surgery, getting overlooked because he is from California…. did not stand in his way, and his desire to succeed no matter what the obstacles have prevailed.

Do you get nervous watching games and if so how do you combat those nerves?

I am a nervous wreck! I chew gum… Wrigley's. I will typically go through at least a pack of gum during the game. My dentist has told me to cut back on the gum but that's easier said than done! I have even had people come up to me and make comments about seeing me on TV at the games and chewing away. I have gotten much better with my game watching. Experience has been able to reduce my stress quite a bit, but I am still a goalie dad!

What is one piece of advice you would give other goalie parents?

Be patient. I feel almost like a hypocrite saying this as Thatcher played in the USHL at 15 and as a freshman at Boston College, was the youngest player in the NCAA… but… goalies typically take longer to develop. Some of it is the goalie taking a tad longer to "get it" and part of it is teams "developing" goalies longer before giving them the reins. Just because other players on your child's team are getting offers from Junior teams, College teams, etc. doesn't mean you need to jump at the first offer presented. You need to make sure it is the "right" opportunity that fits your child best. From a hockey standpoint, a school standpoint, and a life standpoint. Just because it's a "powerhouse" team doesn't mean it's the right fit for your child… you need to find those opportunities that will get good, goalie-specific coaching, good playing experience, and provide a development experience that is preparing them for the next level. My other advice would be to have a hip activation mobility program before and after practice. A proper program could help combat the wear and tear a goalie has on their hips.

Practice Makes Perfect

This section will talk about practice but before we do anything we have to talk about pre-practice, and what we do leading up to practice. What we do prior to practice will be pivotal with respect to maximizing the actual practice time. If you're like most people the actual ice time pales in comparison to the many hours available throughout the day. Therefore it becomes essential that goalies maximize their time on the ice by preparing accordingly. Here are a few tips that might help prepare your goalie for practice.

Pre-Practice

1.   Be Fueled.

Make sure that your goalie is fueled properly for practice so he/she does not fatigue early and starts to drag. This will not only impact variability to perform technique and structure correctly but if they are not successful on the ice and practice and give up more goals than they should this will impact their passion for the position and enjoyment of the game.

2.   Pack Early.

Have your goalie have their bag ready to go long before it's time to leave for the rink. I will never forget when I was a peewee and practice was at 6:00 am, I forgot to pack my skates and my mother was absolutely livid. One suggestion that may help is to have a checklist posted where your goalie's equipment is stored. They can put their equipment in their bag one piece at a time and therefore they have all their gear. What you don't want is for your son or daughter to be scrambling to pack their bag as you call out to them that it's time to leave.

3. Do Homework.

Being able to concentrate while performing a task is especially essential when you're learning new skills. A goaltender with a clear head and an open mind will be more receptive to learn and improve as opposed to a goalie that has their head elsewhere. One of the ways to ensure a clear head is to have homework completed before practice as opposed to waiting until after practice if possible.

4. Be on Time.

I don't know about you but in order for me to have a successful meeting I have to be prepared, organized and on time. Rushing into a meeting without time to settle is a recipe for a bad outcome. Make sure that you're getting your goalie to the rink with plenty of time to get ready for practice. Not only does it give them time to do their pre-practice warm-up but a big part of being on a team and playing sports is interacting and socializing with your teammates. Bringing your goalie just in time or late to practice will deprive them of the opportunity to bond with teammates, prepare properly, and therefore take advantage of their ice time.

5. Warm-Up. *hip activation*

Goalies should have a warm-up routine prior to the time they get on the ice. For some goalies, this is typically provided for them and often the team does a group warm-up prior to getting on the ice. Younger goaltenders should also be doing a pre-practice warm-up and it is a parent's responsibility to learn about what they should be doing and teaching them how to do it. One of the issues that the goalies are confronted with is injuries due to excessive wear and tear of the hips. These injuries include hip impingement and labral tears. To help prevent these injuries goalies should make sure to do hip activation as a core part of their pre-practice warm-up.

6.   Give some space.

Practice is the time for your goalie to get better and although it's great to have your support during games it is not the same for practice. During this time your goal is to not feel that every move they make is being scrutinized and evaluated. Therefore it is best for your goalie that after you deliver them to practice you give them the space needed for them to work on their craft. After you get your goalie set up for practice is a great time for you to get some work done, make a few calls, or even get some reading in. I'm not saying you can't poke your head in and watch some of the practice but hovering over your goalie for 60 minutes, in the long run, is not going to help them progress.

7.   Lower your expectations.   re: coaching in practice

I'll never forget going to my son Joey's first practice as a goalie. I was coming from the Boston Garden where I was the goalie coach for the Bruins and my wife Daniela had taken him to practice. I was excited to see how he did on the ice facing live shots. Before this practice, he had done lessons with me at my training center but we'll talk more about that when we get to the training section of this book. I'll never forget sitting in the stands and watching that practice. Throughout the entire length of the practice, not one coach said one word to Joey. I remember thinking... Could one of the coaches please just simply go up to Joey and tap him on his pads or say something... anything? I learned early as a goalie dad to lower my expectations in practice. Youth hockey organizations simply aren't built to provide for goalies. Most coaches don't know what to say, how to say it, or when to talk to goalies, so many of them simply choose to avoid working with the goalies altogether. Hopefully, your organization either provides a goalie coach or sends their goalies to a goalie development center for training but just don't expect to see someone on the ice working with your son/daughter each practice.

Practice

Now that we have gone over some of the things a parent can do prior to practice it's time to dive into the practice itself. Feeding off lowering your expectations it's important your goalie has a clear understanding of why they are going to practice and what the outcome should be. With a goalie not getting the attention of the other players in practice, a goalie parent can help their son or daughter maximize their time on the ice during practice by providing them some tips. A key note here is that you don't have to be a goalie expert to explain the following eight points and they can continuously be reinforced until they become second nature.

1. Goalies need to work hard, track the puck, and control what they can control in their practice time.

Goalies should be accountable if they are not physically or mentally putting forth the effort to challenge the other players and themselves to improve. Earlier in this book, we talked about the motto "control what you can control" and there's no greater example than controlling effort. Effort has nothing to do with anybody else other than your goalie. It is a decision that is made by the individual that demonstrates personal integrity. Having your son or daughter be able to consistently put the effort in practice after practice will serve as a valuable learning tool for everything that they do in life, from sports to school, to work. They may not have someone on the ice that's pushing them so it'll be up to them to make sure they're working their butt off. Hard work is habit-forming and once it is ingrained in the body it will do nothing other than work hard when it's time to practice. As a parent, knowing when to push and when to ease off is really important. If you push

effort

the work ethic too hard you could turn practice into a negative as opposed to a positive. So my advice is to try to pick the right times and the frequency to encourage hard work on the ice regardless of whether it's a game or practice.

Michael Condon was a goalie that made it to the NHL but it was not an easy path. Undrafted, Michael played prep school hockey at Belmont Hill in Massachusetts and college at Princeton where he had to battle with Sean Bonar for playing time his first three years. As a senior, he took control of the net and after that season joined the Orlando Reign, an ECHL team because of injury. After three weeks he was promoted to the AHL's Houston Aeros, due to another injury, where he was spotted by the Montreal Canadiens and signed to an NHL contract. After one season playing for the Hamilton Bulldogs, he made the team, which is one of the most storied franchises in NHL history. In talking to the Montreal staff one of the biggest reasons why Michael Condon made the Canadiens was his insatiable work ethic. He would routinely beat the coaches to the rink in the morning and leave after everyone else was gone. He was the first guy on the ice and he'd stay at practice until everyone had left. That means after practice he would take shots by whoever wanted to stay out until the very last player had wrapped up their work. He was the perfect complement to superstar goaltender Carey Price in the sense that he always did the extra the team needed and won the support of management, coaches and players.

2. Compete at a high level.

I remember attending my first scouting meeting with the Toronto Maple Leafs. I had no idea what to expect as I walked into the conference room at Trump Towers in Chicago. NHL teams typically hold their scouting meetings at different locations and often around when the team is playing on the road on the West Coast or any destination city. The setup for the meeting had one u-shape of tables, 25 scouts, and management reviewing a list of all the top players in the world for the draft. The one thing that became clear to me early on while listening to the scouts presenting the players was that the competitive level of a player was one of the scout's highest priorities. Therefore a player that may not have been the greatest skater or goal scorer may still be ranked high because of their competition level. This was intuitive to me because I know with all my years of experience how hard it is for a goalie to make it to the NHL. So much adversity and so many challenges have to be overcome that the quality of being extremely competitive is what a goalie is going to need to see this through to give themselves a chance to make it. When a goalie is competing in practice not only are they making themselves better but they're also making their teammates better increasing the difficulty to get scored on. The competition between the goalies and the shooters in practice will elevate the level of everyone and make the team better.

As a parent, there are times we celebrate the hard work of our kids such as school graduations and making teams in tryouts. I was very fortunate as a goalie parent because my youngest son Alex naturally possesses a competitive level. I don't know if it is because he is the younger brother but watching Alex compete whether it was a practice or a game would fill me up with pride. You just knew, no matter what the situation or what he was doing, that kid was going to give his all. I wish I had the magic formula to install that in all the kids that I work with but for Alex, it was just innate. This is why his coaches and teammates always supported him throughout youth hockey because no matter what, they were always able to count on Alex trying his hardest and doing everything he could to keep the puck out of the net and give the team a chance to win.

There is no greater example of an elite goaltender that competed for every single puck in practice than the great Dominik Hasek. As a goalie coach in the NHL, one of the coolest things you get to do is watch the opposing team's morning skate the day of a game. As the goalie coach of the Bruins, I was excited to watch Dominik Hasek in the morning skate the night we played Buffalo because I had a chance to play against him while I was a pro in Europe. I will never forget how he competed for every single puck and rebound in practice the morning of the game. I simply couldn't believe what I was seeing. He was the starting goalie that night but he gave his all in the morning skate because it just was in his DNA to contest every shot heading towards his net. On top of that, he did it again during warm-ups before the game. It was at that point I realized the reason he was able to play at the elite level he played and have the success he had was his refusal to get scored on. He, therefore, became a great example of the importance of competing.

3. Control rebounds and cover or clear loose pucks.

Once again the advice and the lessons that we as parents are teaching our goalies don't have to be based on a deep knowledge of the position albeit mechanics or structure. Controlling rebounds and covering loose pucks is essential for goalies to have success in games. Later in this book, you will read about how to evaluate your goalie and puck retention is a pivotal aspect. The first thing and the best result after a shot on net is for the puck to stick to the goalie and be frozen and therefore there is no rebound. Freezing the puck can come in the form of catching it in the glove or smothering it in the body. By freezing the puck a resulting faceoff will ensue which gives the goalie's team a 50-50 chance to get control of the puck off the draw. The second-best outcome is that the shot at the goaltender results in a rebound and the goalie's team gets possession of the puck. So, therefore, rebound control isn't just putting pucks to the corners but rather putting the puck in a position that the goalie's team gets possession. The third outcome, which is less favorable, is the puck shot on the net is stopped by the goalie and the rebound ends up on the sticks of the opposing team. The least favorable outcome is obviously if the goalie doesn't make the save and the shot ends up in the back of the net.

It is essential goalies focus on not only making the save but also what the result of that save will be, namely the rebound. In an ideal situation, practice is set up so that goalies can track their rebounds and play them out. One issue is that this isn't always the case. Goalies must understand that in some drills there just isn't enough time to track the rebound and play it like in a game situation. Sometimes the shots just come one after another with no time. Here we go back again to control what you can control! The goalie can't control the drill the coaches are running and whether there is enough time to work on rebound control and tracking of the rebounds. Therefore, the goalie has to understand that when there is time to track and play the rebounds they have to do it. There should be no time where a rebound and drill are set up for the players to continue playing out the rebound that the puck isn't contested by the goalie. We can even go back to the last point about competing. This is a great chance for goalies to work on their competitive level in practice and its importance cannot be understated.

4. Stay visually attached to pucks. Follow the puck into your body and away from your body.

i.e., nose on puck

There's a great quote by Pavel Francouz of the Colorado Avalanche and it goes like this. "I do not fear stopping the puck, I fear not seeing the puck". The ability to track a puck and stay visually attached is paramount to success between the pipes. Learning how to watch a puck and how it was released off the stick needs to be practiced over and over again so that it becomes second nature. When I scout, I can determine fairly quickly which goalies continuously lose the puck and have to regain visual attachment. The real good goalies are the goalies whose eyes are just glued to the puck. In a practical scenario, when a shot is taken in practice, the goalie stays visually attached to the puck all the way through the release, the save, and the rebound.

What you will find, particularly with younger goalies is that they will watch the release of the shot but as it gets closer to the body they stop following it just before contact. What this means is that they may not be able to locate the puck as easily off the body and it will make it harder to make the second save. Goalies have to really work at this and train the habit of watching the puck in all three phases of the shot. Once again this is something that as a parent you can help reinforce without being a goalie expert or former hockey player yourself.

5.   Be vocal during situational drills and interact with teammates.

It's amazing how little things in a hockey game matter. At the highest levels whether it's the NHL or the AHL communication between a goalie and their teammates can be one of the small differentiating factors between winning or losing games. A goalie has the opportunity to scan the entire rink from the net. Often teammates end up with their back to the play or engage in a battle where they don't have time to see what else is going on and what the opponent's options might be. A vocal goaltender will be able to shout commands to his teammates which will help them make better decisions and hopefully improve the ability to help the defense defend a rush, fill a passing lane or get the puck out of harm's way and ideally out of the zone.

Building up the skill of communication starts in practice. Goalies need to get in the habit of calling out commands in almost all situations. In games, when the opposing team has control of the puck and is moving through the middle of the ice or the neutral zone, it is helpful when a goalie calls out what type of rush it is. Therefore, if there are three opponents skating down the ice towards the net a goalie repeatedly calls out the numbers 3, 3, 3. The same goes if there are two players on the rush and so on. A goaltender can also identify if it's a 3 on 2, 3 on 1, 2 on 1... and so on. If they anticipate something happening like a drop pass to a trailer the goalie can call out the word trailer multiple times helping their teammates be able to respond faster to what happens and ideally a dangerous opponent.

You can see how much communication helps when a defenseman goes back to play the puck after it is dumped in. Traditionally, goalies will call out what they think is the best option for their teammate. Typically, there are four commands experienced goalies use.

I. Wheel. When a goalie calls out the word wheel while the defenseman is picking up the puck what they are saying is that the player should collect the puck and keep skating with it.

Wheel

II. Reverse. When a goalie calls out the command reverse, what they are in fact saying is they want the defenseman to reverse the direction of the puck back to the strong side of the ice.

Reverse

III. Over. When a goalie calls out the command over this means that their teammate should pass the puck to the opposite side of the ice.

Over

IV. Hold it. When a goaltender calls out the words 'hold it' they are directing their teammate to stop and hold on to the puck as opposed to carrying the puck or passing it up ice. An example of this is when there is a line change going on, the team is trying to get fresh legs on the ice, and there

Hold

Stretch?

is no pressure being applied on the forecheck by the other team. As a goaltender, getting to play the puck and calling out commands becomes more and more important each year. Clean exchanges between goalies and defensemen are essential. The habit of communication will definitely help as time goes on.

There is also a psychological aspect that goes along with being a vocal goaltender. A goalie that boldly calls out commands displays confidence to his teammates, coaches, and the other team. Remember, earlier in this book, we defined confidence as the ability to act. A goaltender that is shouting out commands is therefore acting and thus displaying confidence. The thing about communicating is that it has to be consistent and that consistency starts at practice. If a goaltender is consistently vocal at practice it is clear that they are fully engaged in what they are doing and present in the moment. A goalie that communicates early on in a game is letting everyone in the rink know that they are ready to play and therefore makes a huge statement that they are going to give their best and provide their team with a fully engaged, fully present, confident leader between the pipes.

6.   When the players are participating in on-ice warm-up drills they should do 5 to 10 minutes of their own goalie-specific skating drills at the beginning of the ice session.

As I mentioned earlier, ice time is precious. If you think about it, most youth players only get 2 to 3 hours of ice time to practice during the course of the week. Some teams only practice for 50 to just 60 minutes and therefore maximizing that ice time is essential. One of the most frustrating things goalie parents do is watching their goalies take one knee down while watching explanations by the coaches on player skills or systems that have very little to do with goalies. There are also times during full practices that the team goes down to one end and therefore only utilizes one goal. With one goalie in the net the other goalie usually just stands there and watches or takes a knee and chats with other players who are not involved in the drill. This is an ideal opportunity to take it upon themselves to get better.

As a parent, it is important for you to explain to your goaltender that this is a time where they should be working on their skills while the players are working on their own. There are a couple of things, in particular, a goalie can do and that is to work on their skating and puck handling... two big differentiators between goaltenders. Goalies should have a set of simple skating drills that they can perform anywhere on the ice in a small area that will not impact any of the players or the practice drills going on. A common setup for skating drills is to place the pucks in a shape and then move from spot to spot or in this case puck to puck. The most traditional shape is a triangle because the triangle can symbolize the peak of the crease in the middle and both pucks on either side indicate the 45-degree mark of the crease. A goaltender can vary the skating drills by simply changing the shape of the pucks. Therefore, simply moving pucks into the shape of a square can change the drill. Goalies can make the shape of a triangle, square, hexagon as well as simply making a line or creating letters such as an X or W.

A goalie does not need a coach to set up pucks for them and tell them what they need to do. This is something that they can do on their own whenever there is downtime in a practice. Once again, as a parent, you do not have to be a goalie coach to know how to do these drills and how the pucks can be set. What a goalie should be doing while moving from puck to puck is skating with explosiveness and moving in control. That means when a goalie moves to the spot, just like in a game, every part of their body should be in control and moving as one unit. Therefore, if a goalie is moving from a puck on their glove side to the peak their glove should not trail behind their

* don't trail glove or blocke

body as they move. The same thing goes for the blocker. When a goalie is moving from the blocker side to the glove side the stick and the blocker should not lag behind the body. When the glove or blocker lags it prevents the hips from moving properly and slows down the explosiveness of the goalie. When moving, goalies can simply think about the mantra "head, hands and hips."

There is one secret that I have discovered within the skating drills that can separate goalies from others that are doing the same drills routinely and that is what I call "mogility." Mogility is simply goalie-specific movement combined with agility. So how this works is when a goalie is doing their skating drills and moving spot to spot, they simply add a full pivot (circle) around the puck that they stop at. Therefore, if a goalie is doing a skating drill with their puck in the formation of a box each time they move from one puck to the other they make a full pivot around the puck that they set on before moving to the next puck. While making this pivot they should always be facing up ice. By facing up ice while they pivot around the puck, they will be forced to use both their inside and the outside edge. The reason this is important is that so much goalie skating is done on the inside edges but when the goalie has to leave their crease to play the puck they will need to be proficient on their outside edges as well. This can even apply to a game situation when a goalie ends up off balance and has to regain their control on their skates. Mobility skating, using shapes or letters of pucks over a prolonged period of time can produce great results.

7.   Know the 10-20 rule.

Over the past 10 years in particular there has been a dramatic increase in hip injuries to goaltenders. They primarily come in the form of hip impingement and torn labrums. This is a very real problem due to the blocking techniques all goaltenders use to help them best stop pucks going into the net. Blocking techniques principally consist of butterflies and RVH techniques. The issue comes from repetitive movement over long periods of time and there has been a lot of studies and research done on this It is for this reason I created the 10 - 20 rule to help prevent hip injuries for goaltenders. This may be a rule that you would like to discuss with your goalie and your coach prior to the season.

When I started looking at what I could do as a coach to help prevent injuries for goaltenders I did my own study to get a good understanding of how many times a goaltender goes down in practice. I was coaching in Mannheim, Germany at the time so I started counting how many times a goaltender goes down in a typical practice and that number came out to 125. Those 125 butterflies came during a typical 80-minute practice. If you add on pre-practice, a nice warm-up and post-practice, 125 quickly becomes 200. If you take the butterflies for each practice and multiply them through the course of a season, I determined that my goalies were going to perform 10,000-20,000 practice butterflies in one season. The issue is not only the sheer wear and tear of the hips of performing so many internal hip rotations a year but there is not a corresponding balancing of external hip rotations that would offset the impact. Therefore, I wanted to find a way in which I could limit the number of internal rotations and that's the 10 - 20 rule.

The 10 - 20 rule is very simple to use and there are goalies and coaches that use their own variation to the rule. When a drill starts, that is not a team concept drill such as power plays and penalty-killing, the goalie stays on their skates and does not go down on the first 10 shots of the drill. After the first 10 shots of the drills, the goalie is free to go down and do everything they need to do to stop a shot. After those 10 shots and a combination of 20 shots in total, the goaltender returns to staying on their skates and not going down. The reason why the goalie will stop after 20 total shots are that injuries typically result from when an athlete is fatigued. Stopping at 20 shots you stop the internal rotations and grinding on the hips when the goalie's form is starting to deteriorate within a drill.

The primary detriment to the drill is the perception of the coaches. There is a universal perception that if a goalie is not going down to stop the puck they're not working hard and the coaches want to make sure that the goalies are getting better. The truth of the matter is that when a goalie is on their feet they are working on essential skills that will help them become better goalies. Skating is the foundation of goaltending success and a goalie that can get to their spots and get their feet set has a greater probability of making saves. The 10 - 20 rule emphasizes a goalie's skating, positioning, and ability to get square to a puck. A goalie that is staying on their feet is learning not to simply drop every time the puck is being released. A goalie staying on their feet is working on patience and the ability to read a release and react to a shot. Far too many goalies simply drop on the release of a shot. By using the 10 - 20 rule goalies improve their goalie IQ of reading plays and reading releases. Another tremendous benefit of a goalie trying to stop a puck without going down is the use of the hands. Goalies need to be active with their glove and blocker and keep them out in front of them exactly where they need to be able to make saves which also helps with box control. A concept that will be discussed later in this book. Goalies will also use their stick to make saves on shots along the ice and thus improving their hand-eye coordination and most importantly the ability to control the puck with their stick and direct rebounds where they need to go.

The 10 - 20 rule needs to become the norm in goaltending if we want to protect the hip health of all of our aspiring goalies. The only way to do this is through education and communication and parents become a big part of spreading the news. A coach that thinks a goalie is lazy by not going down every single shot needs to be convinced that this isn't the best way a goalie should be practicing. The easiest analogy to explain to a coach why this is the case is to ask them if they think players should be making full-body contact with each drill throughout practice. Although you'll hear every coach preach that players should finish their checks in a game, if the players finish their checks in practice the coach wouldn't have very many players left at the end of the year that could actually step on the ice. So if the players don't need to finish their checks and practice, why should a goaltender have to go down on every shot?

8.   Create a goaltending department within the team.

In practice, both goalies compete hard to make themselves and the other players better. Competition between goaltenders is encouraged because they will push each other and improve at a faster rate. When the puck drops for a game, they should be supportive of the other goalie because the team depends on the goaltending in which both goaltenders contribute through preparation.

Some goalies are the only goalies on their team while other teams have two goalies. When my kids grew up they always played on teams with two goalies and it was great to see the bond between both of them. Inevitably, they are the only two on the team who play "a different sport" than all the other players, and therefore there is a natural bond that is formed. Some of my kids' best friends even to this day are the goalies that they were paired up with during youth hockey. The first thing goalie partners have to do is create healthy competition. This healthy competition is what's going to make both of them better. By pushing each other in practice it will not only improve their skills but it will also make the team better.

While competing in practice and trying to outdo the other goalie is healthy when it comes to game time they positively should support the other goaltender and the same goes for the parents. When goalies play on a team that is classified as play to win, it is often the coach's decision on whom to play and when. This can be very tough for the goalies to accept and sometimes even tougher for the parents. The challenge of having to compete for ice time and games with the other goalie may just be the most important part of all in the goalie's development. It may not feel like it at the time but in the long run, it forces the goalies to compete and challenges them to bring the focus on a consistent basis. All goaltenders are in the goalie fraternity, and we are all putting ourselves on the line every time we hit the ice. It is not the other goaltender that is determining who plays or not... It is the coach. And in a goalie's world karma is a real thing and you want to make sure that when your goalie is in net that all of his teammates and the parents are supporting them.

Post-Practice

We went over what a parent can do in preparation for practice as well as what kind of advice they can give their goalies for what they need to do during practice... but what about after practice? What is the role of a parent after practice is over? Here are a few tips for what you can do as a parent after the kids have completed practice.

1. Say thank you.

I have always been so fascinated listening to parents complain about their youth hockey coach. For most of us goalie parents the youth hockey coach is a volunteer and not receiving any payment in return for their time. There is also a high probability that the youth hockey coach knows very little about coaching goaltenders and has very little experience in this field. Often a dispute between a parent and a coach is regarding a particular decision that the coach makes in a number of different areas. What often gets overlooked is how many decisions a coach has to make. Whether it's regarding practice... such as how much time should be allotted for skill development or team development? What type of drills to do? How intense practice should be? How much fun time should be included in practice? How much instruction should be strategies? Game decisions such as putting the lines together? Who to play in what spot when and how much? Balancing staying competitive and winning? Pushing the kids without discouraging them. The list never ends but typically an issue comes down to one decision versus the myriad of decisions a coach has to make that causes conflict.

So a simple thank you while the kids skate off the ice just makes it all worth it. I don't live in la-la land and I do realize that some coaches are better than others but that being said everyone's time is valuable and I have a tremendous amount of respect for the coaches that dedicate not only their time but their energy to give the kids a positive experience. Please encourage your goalies to say thank you after each and every practice as this will not only be the right thing to do for the coaches but will be teaching our kids a valuable life lesson.

2. Pack Up.

One of the habits we want to instill in our goalies is to take ownership and accountability of themselves. Once again this is an area where we can control what we can control. Goalie equipment is their tool of the trade and they should treat that equipment with respect and accountability. Therefore, after practice, a goalie should have the same routine of packing their bag in the locker room as they do at home. Whether it's happened to you or you've seen it happen to others, it is frustrating for a parent that has to go back to the rink after they've returned home only to find out their goalie is missing a piece of equipment… or worse than that is finding out days later that they're missing a piece of essential equipment needed for that day's game! If you're anything like me you've been part of those phone calls, group texts or email messages when a parent is scrambling trying to find a piece of their kid's equipment. Parents should discuss this with their kids prior to the season and remind them periodically throughout the year to create great habits when packing their equipment.

3. Time to leave.

One of the enjoyable parts about being on a hockey team is hanging out with the other players in the locker room before and after practice. Although these are important times for social development it also needs to work for the parent. The parent is taking a big chunk of their day to drive their kids to practice and bring them home. I don't think it's fair for the kids to take too much time after practice before leaving the locker room so these allotments of time should be decided in advance. I cannot tell you how many conversations I have been involved in where parents have been so frustrated with how long it took their kids to get out of the locker room. I would suggest you sit down with your goalie and come up with a mutually agreed upon amount of time that they will spend in the locker room after practice before leaving. Having an agreed time will end any potential conflicts down the road and make for better relationships and understanding between a parent and a child.

4. The drive.

Driving home after practice with your goalie is a chance to discuss not only practice but anything that's on their minds. The difference between discussions in the car after practice and discussions after the game is that the emotion factor is not in play. It's funny when I think back as a parent about all the time driving back and forth to the rink and not realizing that this was the greatest of times I have to bond with my kids. For me, driving back and forth to practice without the pressure of driving to a game or maybe the disappointment after a loss was simply the best of times. I really wish I would have known back then how precious that time was because I would give anything to have that time back in the car again with my kids. I know that there are times when there is a lot on a parent's mind and how taking the time to drive the kids to their sporting events can be a true sacrifice. Sometimes it can be frustrating but if you project that frustration on your kids it will impact the experience and therefore decrease their passion to play. As we discussed earlier every kid is different and you must learn the best way to communicate in order to encourage them and spark their curiosity. If you're talking about what happened at practice and discussing how they did is generally a non-emotional conversation. We all want our kids to get the most out of practice and make sure that they are trying their best and working hard to improve while having fun. A parent's role is to fuel the passion. How you pick your words in the car is a big part of how you influence their passion for the position as it will be that passion that pushes them through the adversity that they will inevitably face as a goaltender. I mentioned earlier, as a coach, how gratifying it was to get a thank you as the kids skated off the ice. In the same manner, I think it's important that on the drive home the kids say thank you to their parents. Not only will a thank you go a long way for making you as the parent feel appreciated but it will teach the goalie that having the opportunity to play hockey is not a right, it's a privilege. I know as a parent it sometimes is an awkward conversation about your kids showing appreciation. Being honest and straightforward with kids and letting them know that it is important for them to express their gratitude is keeping it real and only the right thing to do.

5. Unpacking.

Being a goalie coach is different from being a player-coach. You are often in close proximity to the goaltender while teaching them their mechanics and structure. It is often a hands-on proposition. Therefore, goalie coaches will be the first ones to tell you which goalies unpack their gear after practice and which goalies leave their wet gear in their bag until it's time to leave for the next skate. It is important when a goalie gets home that they unpack their gear so that it can dry in time for the next practice or game. Leaving gear in the bag not only will cause the equipment to smell but is also unhygienic and it may lead to a potential rash or infection issues. It doesn't matter what age the goalie is, it should be the goalie and not the parent that unpacks the equipment. Having the goalie unpack their own gear begins the process of teaching them "to pay the price". It only takes a couple of minutes to unpack a goalie bag but the lesson of accountability and control is an easy one to make.

Goalie Parent Interview #3: Mike Rooney

Maddie Rooney is a 1997 born goaltender for the USA National Women's Team and her penalty shot save at the 2018 Winter Olympic which defeated team Canada for the gold medal is an iconic Olympic moment. She was also a member of the 2017 IIHF Women's World Championship gold medal-winning game. A native of Andover, Minnesota she grew up playing both boys and girls hockey on her way to the University of Minnesota-Duluth where she was awarded the 2018 Bob Allen Women's Player of the Year Award. Maddie played the 20-21 season as a member of the PWHPA and holds a Bachelor's degree in business marketing.

When did your daughter decide to be a goalie?

We wanted to get Maddie involved in a team sport and hockey was up and coming in our area. When we were at the registration table we had the choice of whether to play in the boys or girls program and the boys' situation was more established so she started there. Going into squirts, Maddie said she wanted to be a goalie. I asked her why and she just simply said... "I want to stop pucks". The rest as they say is history.

What did you feel about that decision?

We wanted to make sure she really wanted to be a goalie because we knew the commitment level involved. We signed her up for some summer goalie camps and that fall she made the top boys squirt team as a goalie. I was apprehensive at first because Maddie was a strong skater and doing very well with the boy's team. In hindsight, it was a great decision but at the time it was not made without reservation.

What has been the best part of the journey so far?

Knowing the life lessons that you can learn playing a team sport and watching Maddie develop as a person has been the best part so far. Building character, growing in confidence, and staying humble are qualities that were developed playing goalie and hockey and we could not be prouder parents. The icing on the cake was all the great games including of course the gold medal win over Canada at the Olympics. There were so many exciting games from youth to high school and college and playing for the national program and it was great experiencing them as a family.

What has been the most challenging part of being a goalie parent?

Being a goalie parent definitely comes with some stress because the outcome of a game often rides on the goalie's performance. A lot of people see a goal go in but they miss the subtleties of the events that actually occurred preceding the goal. The old ABC Wide World Of Sports intro of "The thrill of victory and the agony of defeat" definitely applies to the world of goaltending!

What were the key aspects of her development that stand out to you?

Maddie was very fortunate to have been in some quality programs but most importantly she was surrounded by great people that cared for her. She also lucked out by having great coaches that believed in her. Playing with both the boys and girls programs was also a key to her achieving what she has accomplished. After playing two years with the girls at High School she played her senior year with the boys and that really helped her get ready for college.

Do you get nervous watching games and if so how do you combat those nerves?

To be honest I am still getting used to it. I sit with my wife and we try to enjoy the game and cheer on the team. I can't say that I am relaxed especially if she is seeing a lot of action but I would say I just try to cope as best I can and being a little nervous just comes with the territory.

What is one piece of advice you would give other goalie parents?

I think the best piece of advice that I could give to goalie parents is not to get down on your kid. At the end of the day, regardless of the outcome of the game, you just have to remember that they are out on the ice trying to do their best. Remembering that they are doing the best they can and interacting with them the same way regardless of the score is a key to being a good goalie parent. We have an expectation level and it's easy to get caught up it but as goalie parents we have to temper our expectations and not let our emotions get the best of us and always be as supportive as we can.

Games

I'll never forget an experience I had with my older son Joey while he was playing for two teams as a peewee. Joey was a goalie for a select team and played out for the town team. One Saturday night, I got a call from the parents of the goalie from the town team telling me that their son was sick and he would not be able to play the next morning. That was no problem, Joey would bring his goalie gear and play in net the next day. What happened to me at that point was pretty funny. I went from being totally relaxed and not thinking much about the game at all to dialing it in: "Okay, what time do I need to get Joey to bed tonight?", "What did he have for dinner?", "What time do we need to wake up in the morning?", "Do I have directions to the rink?", "I better check that bag twice and make sure he had all his goalie gear", "Whom are they playing?", "What time should he eat breakfast before leaving for the game?" It was almost comical how I went from having this laissez-faire attitude to getting my game face on because he was going to be the goalie as opposed to a player.

A goalie can have a tremendous impact on a hockey game. We've all been at those games where the ice is tilted and the result should be one thing but because of the play of one single person on the ice, the result is dramatically different. Look at how Carey Price vaulted the Canadiens in the 2021 Stanley Cup playoffs. It is a hollow feeling as a goalie parent when you see all the other kids dialed into the game and working hard and your goalie is not ready to play and the entire team suffers. Looking at my mindset and the difference between how I prepared my son as a goalie versus a player is a great example of what's necessary for game preparation.

Pre-Game Preparation

Success in a game can be linked to pregame preparation and habits. The parent of a goalie is responsible for doing their part and making sure their son or daughter is ready for game time. This preparation and these habits are very similar to the preparation for practice but because it's a game, there are a few nuances that are different from practice. What preparation for games is important typically comes down to the anxiety that an athlete feels before playing. That anxiety will impact the processes and protocols that are in place before competition. Here are some tips that parents can think about with regards to preparing for a game.

If you have ever had to make a presentation at work in front of all your co-workers and bosses, you probably have a good understanding of what it means to have the jitters. For most goaltenders, managing pregame anxiety becomes an important aspect of their development. I know for me, as a former professional goaltender, pregame anxiety was my biggest opponent. My real opponent wasn't the other team but rather myself and what was in my head. The amazing thing was that I intuitively knew that as soon as the puck dropped in the game and I got my first shot, I was going to be fine but I couldn't seem to wrap my head around this and convince myself before the game. In college and pro, my anxiety started to build up as soon as the coach told me that I was starting the next game. At that time, teams even at the highest levels, didn't provide any support when it came to the mental part of the game. I often think back and wish that I had someone to talk to about pregame anxiety and learned about how to approach it strategically.

As I mentioned, anxiety will differ from one person to the next and as a parent, it is important to recognize how anxiety impacts their child and to make sure that they develop a strategy to help better manage that emotion.

Pregame anxiety can cause goalies to start playing the game in their heads long before it's time to drop the puck. The impact of over-thinking the game is that it will fatigue the goaltender mentally and they will not be as sharp come game time. There are countless books authored by performance coaches on this subject but I can offer a couple of strategies that I have found to work well with goaltenders in this situation.

1. The first strategy is breaking down with your goaltender what they are feeling before a game.

This feeling is often referred to as butterflies. So what exactly are the butterflies? Butterflies is that feeling that you have inside your stomach that comes from nervousness, the heart rate starts to speed up and the body temperature rises. Ironically, the same sensation also comes up when someone is excited about something. Therefore, if we can explain to our kids that butterflies and nervousness are the same things as excitement we can change their inner self talk to interpret their anxiety as excitement. So when a goalie says they are nervous, they can be made to understand it as a form of excitement. Thereby, turning a negative word into a positive one. The goaltender that repeatedly utters that they are nervous can now replace that with they are excited to play the game.

2. The second strategy that you can use with your goalie is to simply ask what is important in life.

I'll never forget a speech made by Coach Harold Kreis while I was a goalie coach of Adler Mannheim. We had just lost the night before, after holding a 5-2 lead with 12 minutes remaining in a game that would have clinched the DEL Championship, the top professional league in Germany. As we sat in the locker room, I was anxiously waiting to hear how Harold was going to address the team and get them mentally ready to play the next game which would now be a sudden death game to determine the champion. He stood in the middle of the locker room and quietly and calmly started asking questions from individual players. His questions were not hockey-related by any means. He would ask a player how his wife was doing. He asked the next player about his kids and the player after that about his parents. After a few minutes, it was clear why he was asking these questions. Although the team was extremely disappointed by not winning the championship the night before, what Harry was able to do was to remind them that there were much more important things in life than winning or losing a hockey game. For us as parents, our kids need to understand that they are playing a game and that there are more important things in life than winning or losing a game.

3. A third strategy would simply ask "what would you rather be doing?"

Typically, most of them would love playing hockey and love playing the games so if you identify that they are having some issues with pregame anxiety, you can reframe how they look at things by asking: "If you are not going to go play in this hockey game, what would you rather be doing?" At that point, I think you'll find their response as "I would rather be going to this game". Playing games is exciting and challenging and you get to do it with some of your best friends. It's why we put in the practice time, watch the games on TV and play NHL on Xbox. Playing games allows a goalie to measure where they are at and identify what they need to work on to improve. As a parent, you know you may be nervous about making a speech in front of your entire company but, as soon as you get started, you just settle in and start to roll. It's no different for a goalie in the sense that after they get their first shot they settle in and play their game.

4. A fourth strategy is to teach your goalie the SPIN system.

SPIN stands for Systemic Positivity Inspiring Narrative and it is the system that we teach at the Greatness Lab Training Center located at the Stop It Goaltending headquarters' building named the Pad in Woburn, MA. SPIN is easy to use and can reap immediate rewards. If you practice spin enough, it can become second nature. Spin consists of three elements, (1) Posture, (2) Breathing, and (3) Self-talk. The combination of these elements becomes a powerful tool.

POSTURE
BREATHING
SELF-TALK

Posture is the quickest way that someone can change their mindset. To prove how a change of posture can have a dramatic impact on how you feel, simply stand with your head down and your shoulders slouched while leaning slightly to one side. See how this posture makes you feel; if you're like me, it will make you feel apathetic, lazy, and far from being confident. Now, pull your shoulders back, bring your head up, allow your chest to go out, and put your hands on your hips. Yes, it's pretty close to assuming the Superman pose and it makes you feel pretty powerful.

The second part of SPIN is breathing. To think about how breathing is so important, all you have to do is watch a basketball player driving the hoop and getting fouled on their way to the basket. After they get up and go to the foul line, the referee will give them the ball so that they can take their free throws. What is the first thing that a basketball player is going to do? 100% of the time they are going to take long deep breaths. Remember, they have been up and down the court and therefore their breathing is quicker than they like so they need to slow down their breathing rate which will, in turn, impact the central nervous system which is what they will need to have for them to make successful free throws. SPIN at the G-Lab teaches eight different breathing methods for different situations and there are more videos to help to breathe online than you can shake a stick at. The most simplistic and easy-to-use breathing technique is a simple, even, long breath in through the nose and long breath out through the mouth.

The third component of SPIN is positive self-talk. Look, we talk to ourselves all day long and I read once that we have up to 60,000 thoughts a day. What we need to do is make sure that the self-talk is positive and not negative. There is a great expression that says, "you are what you think." The goalie should be filling themselves with positive self-talk because positive self-talk will be able to drown out those negative thoughts that may creep in. One simple exercise that I use to teach self-talk is when I sit in my office with a goalie and ask them to remember a series of numbers that I call out. At first, I simply tell them the exercise is that I will call out numbers and after I call them out they have to write them down on a piece of paper. After we've done that once, I talk to them about self-talk and the use of a performance statement that was discussed earlier in this book. Now, as I call out the numbers, the goalie talks to themselves and repeats their performance statement over and over while at the same time I'm calling out numbers. Yes, you guessed it, the recollection of the numbers that I called out is dramatically less than when they listen to the numbers without repeatedly saying their performance statement. Teaching your goalie SPIN is great but using SPIN just once in a while will not produce the results as if using SPIN was part of their regular preparation. SPIN can be used the night before a game, the morning of the game, before going on the ice, and even before a face-off.

If you want to see a quick version of what SPIN looks like just check out Philadelphia Flyers' Carter Hart before he steps foot on the ice. Typically, as an NHL team comes out onto the ice before a game they are led by their starting goaltender. This has been a tradition for years and it is no different in

Philadelphia. When Carter Hart is starting the game he is the first in line coming onto the ice but he does something that a lot of goalies do not do. Right as he gets to the door and before he steps foot on the ice he stops in his tracks, changes his posture, takes a deep inhale and exhales, states his inner performance statement, and only then does he step foot onto the ice with his teammates to follow.

5. A fifth approach is a scaled-down version of SPIN and the strategy revolves around simply stating 3 words. Those three words are "play to win."

PLAY
TO
WIN

Yes, you are correct, "play to win" can be a performance statement. When discussing performance statements I generally recommend that the performance statement consists of two parts. Play to win is singular in nature but means so much to a goaltender. If we break down the meaning of play to win it carries a lot of weight and means a lot to how a goaltender is going to play the game because when you play to win you're not thinking about your stats, you're not thinking about the goal that just went in, you're not thinking about how you look, you're not thinking about who's watching, you're not thinking about whether you're going to play the next game or the other goalie is going to play the next game and you're not worried about scouts, scholarships, or accolades. What you are, is singularly focused on helping your team win the game and this drowns out all else and can help a goalie stop over-thinking what's going to go into their performance.

Now that we have gone over several options in which a parent can help their goalies deal with pre-game anxiety, it's time to review the rest of our pregame preparation. Remember that pregame preparation starts from the time a goalie knows that they are starting a game and it is important for a parent to understand this and monitor their goalie and the processes that you both have in place leading up to the contest. You will see that the protocol is very similar to practice preparation but just with the nuances because of the upcoming game. Here are a few tips that you might find helpful.

1. Sleep.

One thing you're going to want to make sure of is that your goalie is well-rested before the game. I learned a long time ago that it is the sleep two nights before the game that is most important. Over the years I've listened to several presentations about sleep and its value. It has always struck me when the experts speak about getting a good night's sleep two days before the competition. Intuitively, I would think it is the sleep the night before the game is most important.. Of course, this doesn't mean that the sleep the night before the game isn't important but it does exemplify the importance of the previous night. The one other sleep that is incredibly important, and this applies mostly to older goaltenders, is the pregame nap. A pregame nap can make or break a performance. A pregame nap should last anywhere from 30 to 90 minutes but any more than that as it can cause the goalie to wake up groggy and not feel right heading into the game. The pregame nap and how long that nap is a very personal thing for each player. Goalies have to experiment with nap time and what length of time makes them feel the best after they wake up. It is not only the length of a nap that is important but how many hours before the game that the nap is taken. Goalies can keep a log of when they napped and how long which will help them figure out what works best for them. What is also important is where they slept and how dark the room was. A lot of experts will tell you not to nap in your bed and not in a blackened-out room. Once again napping protocol for each goaltender should be based on their experience.

2.   Be game fueled.

Eating properly for games is similar to practice but carries more weight because practice does not have a win, tie, or loss associated with it. Later on, in this book, you'll be able to read more in-depth about how to feed your goalies. Pregame fueling traditionally starts the night before the game and ends just before the game. Feeding the body the night before the game is simply the start. Depending on the game time fueling should be done on game day accordingly. You must look at your traditional meal times as well as snacks. Your last meal before the game will be different depending on the age of your goaltender and typically there is a snack in between that final pregame meal and the start of the game. Once again, just like sleeping, you and your goalie will be able to figure out exactly the type, timing, and amount of fueling that works best for them and their ability to perform.

3.   Pack early.

Packing early for a game is a little different than for practice. What I like to suggest to parents is that the goalies pack their gear up long before it's time to go to the rink. Let's imagine there's a game at 5:00 pm in the afternoon. If a goaltender puts their gear in their bag in the morning of the game when it comes time to get ready to leave you will not run the risk of having to wait to pack the bag. With very young goaltenders I still believe that they should be packing their bags but should do so with the oversight of one of their parents. This teaches accountability for what they are doing without running the risk of you getting to the rink only to find out something has been left behind. A goaltender should be packing their bag themselves and follow the same protocol on how they pack their bag so it can be done in a method that can be repeated time and time again. A goaltender will have a clearer head and do a better job packing their bag in the morning of the game as opposed to when they are just about to leave.

4. Do the work.

Most of the time games are on the weekend until you get to the higher levels. To be successful on the ice a goaltender needs a clear head and any outstanding responsibilities such as homework or chores should be done before leaving for the rink. The one thing that you don't want is for your goalie to be thinking about other things they need to do instead of thinking about helping their team win the game. That being said, it is also a good idea for parents to take care of what they need to do so when it's time to leave for the game they've got their things to do checked off and can simply relax and enjoy watching their kid play. If a parent is all stressed out about what they need to do on the drive to the game and the drive home it'll take some of the enjoyment away from the experience and can increase the tension level playing the game and therefore impact pregame anxiety.

5. Know where you are going and plan.

It is important to get your goalie to the rink on time the day of a game so what time to arrive should be thought out in advance. The first part of planning is knowing where the rink is and how to get there. Most parents have a GPS that helps a great deal but you also need to think about the time of the game and potential traffic issues that may occur. The age of each goaltender and the level that they are playing at will be determining factors on what time you need to get to the rink. You should consider allowing yourself an extra 15 to 30 minutes just in case something unexpected happens en route to the rink. It is not good for a goaltender to be squeezed for the time after they get to the rink. They should have time in the locker room, get warmed up, and have plenty of time to put their gear on.

6. Pregame warm-up can either be the same as a pre-practice warm-up or have its twists.

One element of a pregame warm-up versus a pre-practice warm-up that may be different is visualization. A goalie, prior to a game, should spend a few minutes visually watching themselves make saves as a precursor to their actual performance. If you have a chance you can check out some great video clips on YouTube of Braden Holtby and Connor Hellebuyck of them visualizing the game as part of their warm-up routine. The brain is an amazing piece of hardware and the brain cannot differentiate between what is real and what is visualized. The easiest way to understand this is to think of dreaming. When you wake up from a dream you often can't believe how real it felt. You could be out of breath or sweating because your body is reacting as if the dream happened. The same thing goes for visualizing saves a goalie is going to make in a game. The brain doesn't realize that it didn't happen. I often recommend that goalies have a prepackaged reel of saves that they run through in their head as part of their pregame warm-up. It doesn't have to be more than a couple of minutes but it is an exercise that can be pre-planned.

YouTube

7. Stop the madness.

Goalies are well-known for having superstitions and needing to do certain things to get themselves in the right mental state to play the game. I know as a goalie myself it was something that I took very seriously. Superstitions come in the form of always going through a certain door, or sitting in a specific spot in the locker room, or going out onto the ice a certain way. I think it's extremely important to understand the difference between superstition and habits. A superstition is needing to park in a certain spot in the parking lot at the rink while a habit is putting on your left skate before your right skate. In differentiating the two situations putting on one skate prior to the other is something that can be controlled and become second nature. Parking at a specific spot in the parking lot is something that is out of your control and for me falls into the superstition realm. Habits, sometimes referred to as anchors, allow goalies to feel comfortable and help calm them down but when a goalie starts getting caught up in a whole bunch of superstitions it can start to become distracting and sometimes overwhelming. Goalies will often use anchors on game days either on the ice or off it. These anchors are things that they can control and remind them it's game day. A good example of an anchor is tapping of the goal posts prior to the opening face-off of a game. Maybe the tap allows the goalie to say "It's game time, let's go" and they are ready to play. The key is not confusing anchors or habits to superstitions.

Anchors

If I could go back as a goaltender I would get rid of all the superstitions that I used to have because they used to make it as difficult as one compounded on top of the other. I wish I just had my habits prior to the game that would have helped me get in the right state of mind before getting on the ice. My son Joey at one point was going down the same path as me with a bunch of pregame superstitions until he found a way to stop the madness. He started identifying anything that could become superstitious and immediately did the opposite. Therefore, if he parked in a specific spot at a game and they won he would intentionally park in a different spot the next game. Therefore, he identified what could become a superstition and stopped it in his tracks. I use this strategy when I go watch my kids play. I used to get caught up even as a parent in little superstitions thinking for some unknown reason that this would help them succeed and play well. And now I do the opposite of anything that could be deemed superstitious from where I sit to what I wear. Not only do I use this philosophy when going to my kids' games but I use it every day as well and it sure makes things easier for me.

74

8. Give some space.

A lot of times when parents are going to the rink they have nothing to do other than hang out with them until it's time to go to the locker room. All this makes sense if none of the other players are around but it may not be the best advice when they are. Once a goalie is at the rink they should integrate with their teammates. Therefore, I don't think standing with your child in one area while their teammates are hanging out somewhere else and talking is the best course of action. I would encourage goalies to hang out with the players that they are about to go to battle with. This is their time and a great opportunity for them to bond and grow closer as teammates. Parents will get their one-on-one time with their kids in the car to the rink and from the rink but once they get to the rink they should just be kids and hang out with their buddies.

9. Flip the switch.

At some point for every athlete they have to learn when to flip the switch and what that means is that they have to put their game face on. What flipping the switch or putting your game face on means is that it is time to focus on the game and to put the blinders on distractions. Every athlete when they play will put themselves in a state of mind where they are playing "in the moment". What becomes important to each individual is when and how they flip the switch and this is something as a parent that you can help your child figure out.

One thing you don't want to do is flip the switch too early. If you get focused too early before a game you will drain precious energy that needs to be saved for competition. That doesn't mean doing the right things like not going swimming before a game or overexerting yourself so you have energy for the game or anything like that. It's when you get in the zone and are ready to compete. An athlete will experiment with this for a long time until they find the right time for them. Talking about flipping the switch is something that you can do as a parent to explain the importance of concentration and focus and the impact it will have on the results.

While I was playing pro hockey in Switzerland, I played with a forward by the name of Bobby Logan. Bobby played at Yale University, in the American Hockey League and earned some games in the NHL as well. One day, we were just sitting around talking about game preparation and what each other did to get in the zone. What Bobby told me is something I'll never forget, he explained that he didn't think much about the game at all until the national anthem. With not thinking about the game prior to the national anthem he saved his mental energy for when he needed it the most... game time. Therefore, when the anthem started to play you could physically see in his face that he had flipped the switch and was ready to play. It was a great learning moment for me because I spent so much time before the game over-thinking and worrying about playing and what the outcome might be. Bobby taught me that I could relax and be myself up until game time but when that anthem came over the speakers it was all business and time to compete.

With Bobby's advice in mind, I needed to find my trigger and when to flip the switch. I found that waiting for the national anthem wasn't enough time for me to get in the zone and be ready to play, so I had to find my own switch and I found it by putting on my mask prior to going on the ice. As soon as I put my mask on and it was time to head out of the locker room and get on the ice, it was time to compete. I envisioned putting on my mask the same way a superhero puts on their mask. Putting on my mask was almost like getting into character for an actor and I would feel that my mask allowed me to have the superpowers necessary to go out on the ice and give

trigger to flip the switch

76

my team a chance to win. I wish I had learned at an earlier age how to use triggers and when to flip the switch. By not getting myself ramped up too early I was able to enjoy my time more prior to the games and especially in the locker room with my teammates.

At the youth hockey level, there's traditionally not a national anthem before each game and therefore this will not apply in exactly the form Bobby Logan uses. Maybe flipping the switch when a goalie puts on his mask is not the right time for him or her either but the concept can be the same... just the actual switch will be different. A goalie can have their switch such as walking into the rink, walking out of the locker room doors, stepping on the ice, or even cheering at the crease right before puck drop. It is up to every athlete to experiment with when to flip the switch so that they know when the right time is for them and their body and mind can be accustomed to when that is going to happen and reap the rewards of being an athlete in the zone.

10. Lower your expectations.

If you remember from the pre-practice section I also said the same thing... to lower your expectations. Look, we all want our kids to win and have success. It's only natural. But if you want your goalie to succeed in the long run they need to face adversity they need to overcome losses and bad goals. Believe it or not, there is so much good that can come due to failure on the ice. It is that failure that is going to fuel them in the long run and drive them to get better. Therefore, in all reality, anything that happens on the ice is going to be good. If they win and your son or daughter plays well... good... If they lose and your son or daughter does not play well… good.

If you have a minute to look up Jocko Willink on YouTube it will be well worth your time. You will find a two-minute clip from one of his podcasts named "GOOD." Jocko Willink is a decorated Green Beret and recognized as one of the world's top motivational speakers on leadership. In this quick video, he goes over a couple of situations where his platoon members tell him about a problem they are having and his response is always the same... good. The reason he says good is that he recognizes it as an opportunity for them to grow and without having the issues they wouldn't be able to grow. The only way a goalie can get better is to get scored on because by getting scored on they will have to figure out how to stop the puck in that situation. It may not be the next time they see the same shot or the next time after that but eventually, they will figure out how to stop it.

A parent that is relaxed about the potential outcome of a game will help their goalie also be relaxed going into the game. A parent that is nervous with high expectations about the performance can negatively impact their goalie by putting more pressure on them than there has to be. Therefore, if parents enter the game with the attitude that whatever is going to happen is going to be a good thing then they can also enjoy the game more. Now I'm not going to sit here and say this is an easy thing to do. As parents, we have so much love for our kids and want so badly for them to be happy and having fun. We all know that winning is surely a lot more fun than losing but I encourage you to play long ball on this one and hopefully it will allow you to enjoy the games more.

Game Time

To be successful in anything in life you have to be consistent. If you talk to any coach they will tell you they want a goalie that they can trust. But what exactly does that mean... trust. Trust for a coach in his goalie is knowing that that goalie is going to be prepared and ready to play. That the goalie is going to put the team first and play to win that game. The goalie is going to compete on every puck and never give up on a play. Consistency is also important when it comes to how a parent approaches game time. Parents cannot fluctuate and how they carry themselves interact with other parents and coaches at the rink. Coaches like to know what they are going to get from the goalies but also their parents as well. The last thing you want is that a coach is leery or questions your intentions as a parent. Equally as important is that your goalie also knows what to expect from their parents and therefore they can concentrate on doing what they need to do on the ice and not worry about what might be going on in the stands. As a goalie parent, I can tell you that finding my way at the rink was not easy. I've gone through many different stages of how I wanted to approach what I did at the rink on game day.

If you ever talk to my wife Daniela and ask her if I'm competitive she will laugh out loud. She always teases me about how competitive I am, even playing around with the kids at the house, either in the basement or in the garage, playing ping pong or shooting hoops in the driveway. I would like to think that my competitiveness has been transferred on to my children because I think the drive to compete is extremely important concerning development. The one thing that was hard for me as a parent was to understand that when my kids were on the ice, on the court, or in the field... that I wasn't competing... they were.

In my son Joey's case I ended up being the head coach of his youth hockey teams. I found it easy as a parent to watch him play while I was coaching because I wasn't solely focused on him and his performance because I had a whole team to concentrate on. If I was engulfed in the game and busy trying to help all the kids I would not be so fixated on every little thing that he did. This made it more enjoyable I believe for both of us. When Joey started at the local high school as a freshman my expectations were not too high. In each game, I was able to implement the strategy I offered a little earlier and had the mindset that anything that happened on the ice was good. Although I wasn't coaching I was relaxed and comfortable watching the game regardless of the outcome.

When Joey went to prep school and all of a sudden was being watched by colleges and listed on NHL Central Scouting as a potential NHL draft pick, everything changed for me. I lost my perspective of anything that happens is good and all I wanted was for the puck not to end up in his net. I would stand by myself in the corner of the rink with my headphones on, listening to Jack Johnson to calm me down and watch the game without interacting with anyone. I often thought it was so intense for me that I would have been better off sitting in the car in the parking lot until the game was over. So there I was at the game watching my son and my wife sitting without her husband and instead of sharing this fun experience, we were at opposite ends of the rink. I regret not having the opportunity to get a redo on this. I wish I could have put myself in the mindset that it wasn't me competing and that anything that happened was good and I would have sat with Daniela and enjoyed the games.

That changed during Joey's second year at Arizona State University. The Sun Devils were visiting Boston College, in our stomping grounds, and I had a bunch of family coming to the game. I was nervous because Boston College is a powerhouse and being a new and upcoming team ASU was going to be up against it. A few minutes before game time I was about ready to head to the corner of the rink and put my headphones on when Daniela said that there was no way that she was going to watch this game sitting with my family, while I stood alone across the way. Daniela demanded that we will watch the game together, cheer for ASU and have fun watching our son play this game. It ended up being a great game and Joey played extremely well. Our whole group was in "fan mode", including me. From that point on I started watching both our boys' games together with my wife. It has made for so many great moments and brought us closer together by allowing us to share this time and instead of being stressed by the games they are now a fun and enjoyable experience that we can share. I am not telling you that I am not nervous anymore but I found a way to deal with my anxiety so I can enjoy these special moments when both our boys are playing.

One part of fan mode that often surprises people that sit around Daniela and me is that we cheer when the opposing goalie makes a great save. We do this for a couple of reasons and I believe the first is that we are so engulfed in the world of goaltending and proud of all the kids that play the position. We both recognize that it takes a lot of courage and confidence to go down the path and we have a great amount of respect for the kids that put themselves on the line each and every game. Therefore, we simply want all goalies to play well. Nothing would suit us better than watching a 0-0 hockey game every night. Therefore, when either our son or the opposing goalie makes a great save we cheer them on. The second reason we support the opposing goaltender is that we believe in karma and treating people a certain way consistently will bring good karma in the future. If you are like us and believe in karma feel free to cheer for both goalies, it makes you feel good.

1. Where do I sit?

Now that you know that I sit with my wife Daniela at games, where to sit may sound like a trivial decision but I think it is an important one. First off, I recommend sitting at the same spot the entire game. My suggestion to goalie parents is to pick a spot somewhere in the stands at the blue line of the first-period defensive zone. This allows you to see the front of your goalie and enjoy the action with a good view of your son or daughter.

I know that some parents like to stand right behind the glass but think that they will be right on top of their child. The easiest way to explain this to parents is by putting them in the same environment in the workplace. I would think that most people would not like to be sitting at the desk at the office and having their boss a few feet behind them standing up and staring at them the entire time they are working. Well, this is what it's like for a goalie. As they are on the ice trying to concentrate on stopping a puck and helping their team win and their parents are right over their shoulder watching everything they do. I don't think an employee likes it when their boss stands over their shoulder and is watching everything that they do while they try to do their job. What about if you are at work and your boss is not only standing behind you but also offering their opinion every time you do something. There is no difference between that and a parent standing behind the goalie every time they make a good save or give up a bad rebound. I completely understand the intent is an honorable one to be there to support your goalie while they are out on the ice but this is something that they are going to have to do on their own. Figuring it out is a big part of being a goalie and sometimes the kids have to figure it out on their own.

Once you pick a spot, try to stay there the entire game. If you want to be there to support your child, it is important to stay in that spot. What I found with my kids is that when they got on the ice they took a look around and spotted where we were sitting. They then have comfort and knowing where we were and then they can go about their business stopping pucks. I would also recommend that you do not switch ends after each period. If you do so your son or daughter is going to have to look around and try to find your new location. This is part of when I say it's important to be consistent as a parent and having your routine of where you sit and staying at that spot will help create that consistency.

Once you have found a spot and created a routine you have to decide how you want to enjoy the game. Some parents like to sit with the other parents while others would prefer to sit or stand-alone. Either way is fine as long as it's consistent. If you are going to hang out with the other parents you should do this regardless of whether your child is the star of the game or it doesn't go as well as hoped. The same goes for if you are going to stand alone. Although I mentioned how Daniela and I now sit together, I am also fully aware that sometimes the moms like to sit together and chat as well as the dads enjoy watching the game together and hanging out. Regardless of whether you sit alone or together, with the moms or the dads, whether things are going well or not should not determine how you interact with the other parents.

Goalie parents often feel a lot of responsibility to the team that their goalie plays well but it should not impact how you interact socially with the rest of the parents. If you are social in nature and like to interact and talk a lot, interaction should not be impacted by the score of the game or the performance of a kid. Once again this is an area that I believe should be consistent. If you are quiet in nature and do not interact much with other people then that shouldn't be impacted by game results. Just remember it's not the parent that's playing the game, it's the kids and their performance should have no impact on how the parents interact amongst themselves.

I stated earlier that everyone in the rink knows how the goalie played because they have such an impact on the outcome of the game. I think it is important for goalie parents to be cognizant of the fact that their child's performance is something everybody generally recognizes. If you watch any game in the NHL they award the 3 stars of the game at the conclusion. More often than not you will find that one of the stars of the game goes to a goalie. Therefore it is clear that goalies often get a lot of attention and accolades for how they play. As a goalie parent, you want to make sure that you stay even keel about your kids' performance and all of the ups and downs where one minute they can be the star and the next minute could be the goat. The parents must try not to get caught up in the excitement of a big win and inversely a big loss.

2.   How to react after a goal?

We've already determined that most goalies, especially the younger ones know exactly where their parents are sitting. What you may find in a young goalie is the habit of looking up at their parents immediately following a goal. Therefore, if you want your goalie to stay calm and composed after giving up a goal you must do the same thing. Making a face or even throwing your hands up is going to add stress to your goalie and stress only tightens up muscles and diminishes confidence. If you show your son or daughter that the goal was no big deal then that will translate to them and allow them to stay calm and get ready to stop the next shot. Remember, it is at this point that the "never get beat twice" mantra kicks in and the focus has to immediately be on getting ready to stop the next puck.

I remember how quickly my older son Joey looked at me after a goal when he was young. It took me a while to figure out that this was a key component to his enjoyment of the position and that I needed a strategy. If you remember, I was coaching his team at the time and the first thing I said to myself was not to show any frustration or disappointment in my face. Of course, all goalie parents know that every goal that goes in feels like you let it in yourself but we can't let them know that. Therefore, I adapted the routine of clapping my hands and saying things like "no problem boys, we are going to get the next one". My theory was that my actions showed that the goal was not a setback and my energy and enthusiasm were looking forward and not back. I do think this helped my son a lot and eventually, he stopped looking at me after goals. As we know all kids are different, my younger son Alex was not like this at all as he did not look for me after a goal and just dialed in and got ready to play.

3. Make sure you know the expectations of playing time. Whether it is an equal rotation or play to win system, the goalies and parents should all understand the coach's philosophy to eliminate any issues throughout the season.

We all know how important communication is. This is never more present than when issues arise that could be prevented by the coach and the goalie parents communicating with each other. First off, you have to know whether the team is a play-to-win team or an equal play team. If you sign up for a play-to-win team, then ice time will be rewarded based on performance, not based on the fact that everyone plays equally on the team. The rules are pretty simple on a play-to-win team and by accepting that spot you need to also be able to accept that your goalie could end up a backup for that team as opposed to a starter and therefore may receive less ice time than what you envisioned.

An equal play team guarantees that the goalies will play equal amounts and one will not be favored over another because they perform at a higher level. The one thing that you have to keep in mind if your son or daughter is playing for an equal play team is that coaches can divide that ice time how they please. That means they may split the game 50/50 right down the middle with one goalie playing the first half and the other goalie playing the second half of the game. Sometimes a coach will play one goalie in the first period and then replace him or her only to put them back in net for the second half of the third period. Typically a coach uses this method when one goaltender is considerably stronger than the other.

Another approach is that the coach plays the same goaltender the first half of every game and the other goaltender the second half of every game. Coaches that use this methodology typically believe that the goaltender that plays first will help them get off to a better start and keep the game competitive before putting the other goaltender in and sometimes the coach thinks the opposite way and believes it would be better to put the stronger goalie in the second half because that is when the game is on the line. We will get into this a little bit later in this book but I would prefer that the goaltenders rotate both starting the game and ending the game so that they can experience both parts and develop as goalies.

Before the season starts a good idea for a goalie parent is to discuss with the coach concerning how he or she plans on utilizing the goalies. It is not a good idea to have this discussion once the season has started and you are unhappy or questioning the coach's methodology and use of the goalies. Therefore, a casual conversation prior to the season is a great idea and you can follow up that conversation with a quick email that highlights the key points of the conversation while also thanking the coach for their explanation and their dedication to the kids. If there comes a time during the course of the season when there is an issue regarding the utilization of the goaltenders you can always refer to that email which will make you feel better that you did the right thing and understood what was going to happen before the season got underway.

4. Goalies should be supportive of teammates including the other goalie.

Whether the goalie is playing on a play-to-win team or equal play team they must support the other goaltender. Having a partner that understands the position and the demands of that position is an important part of the experience of being a goaltender. Once again the goaltender intends to do everything they can to help their team win. If a goaltender is in the net then they can make saves keeping the team in the game and giving them a chance to win. Unfortunately, a backup goalie is not like a third-line left-wing or third pairing defenseman because those players get to play in the game. The backup goalie may not have the opportunity to play the entire game but he or she can have an impact as well by bringing positive energy to the team.

What a backup goalie can do is be supportive of their teammates including the goalie in the net. They can cheer, celebrate and simply engage in the game. A distracted backup goalie whose body language and social interactions are meant to demonstrate the dissatisfaction of not being in the game is a detriment to the team and therefore not going along with the purpose of all teammates to do whatever they can for the team. By no means am I saying that this is easy as it can be frustrating, particularly on a play-to-win team, to be sitting on the bench. Of course the same goes for the parents of the goalie that's not playing. The goalie parents cannot be sitting in the stands disinterested and more importantly making discouraging or disparaging comments about the goalie. The easiest way to put it in perspective is how you would expect other parents to be when your child is between the pipes.

When it comes to who's playing and who's not I've heard the same comment from parents from the time I started coaching. They always say the same thing…" the other parents tell me that my kid should be playing". I understand that it can be a difficult situation but my response is always the same… "What do you think the other parents are going to tell you?" It would be very difficult for parents to talk to another parent and say "you know I agree with the coach that your kid isn't playing and the other goalie is playing because I think he gives us a much better chance to win". The bottom line is that your son or daughter is not playing that game and whether you agree with it or not you should be consistent in your attitude and approach and support the team by cheering everyone on.

Watching the Game

Some goalie parents have a lot of hockey knowledge while others have very little experience in hockey. By no means do I think a goalie parent is obliged to study goaltending and learn about the techniques and structures involved. Some goalie parents are former goalies, hockey players, or have a passion for the position and learn about goaltending because it is something interesting to them and want to learn. There are plenty of books parents can purchase which will teach them an awful lot about how to play the position. If you are not a hockey aficionado, here are some of the things to look for while watching the game.

1. Warm-up.

I don't know if you're anything like me but if I miss the first few minutes of a movie I have absolutely no interest in watching the rest. I feel the same way about a hockey game. I need to see the warm-up. As someone that has earned a living by scouting hockey goalies, I can tell you one thing… a scout will be watching the warm-up. The warm-up will give you a good idea about what kind of goalie you're looking at including things like their hand-eye coordination and even their personality and character. A reminder once in a while to your goalie that warm-ups are important is a good idea because getting in the habit of having a good warm-up is a habit that could pay dividends in the long run.

The length of a warm-up is different when you move up in hockey. Typically a youth hockey warm-up is going to last three minutes. You see it all the time when a goalie gets on the ice and they are starting the game after a quick lap or two it is time to get in the net and quickly do some skating. The players set up the pucks to start warm-up. If two goalies will be splitting the game, both goalies will need to see some shots during warm-up. When one goalie is in then the other goalie should be off to the side doing some skating drills. If only one goalie is playing in the game and there is only three minutes total to warm up don't worry if your son or daughter is the backup and they don't get any shots. Although this would be great that they got shots as well it just isn't a lot of time and warm-up should be catered for the goalie that will be playing the game. It is important for the kids to recognize this and that there is an understanding of how warm-up is going to be handled.

2. Dropping the puck.

There's a great expression that coaches use all the time about teams that do not get off to a good start in a game…"My team did not show up on time". A good goalie is going to get off to a strong start at the beginning of a game. A couple of quick goals and the team will be chasing all game long. The reason a parent needs to watch the start of a goalie is to be able to identify if it is an issue and to help find solutions on how to consistently start on time. Starting on time consists of two elements, physical and mental. The two are often tied into each other and it is a combination in equal parts that will allow a goaltender to get off to a good start each and every game.

When you think about the physical component of getting off to a good start you have to look at all the pregame preparation that is done starting with sleep, nutrition, and hydration. If all of those are in check then take a look at the physical part of their warm-up prior to the game and make sure that what they are doing is going to get them ready for the game. The next thing to look at is the actual on-ice warm-up prior to the game. Are they maximizing their time in the few minutes they have to get ready in order to start the game well? If the physical side checks all the boxes then it is time to check the mental side of the game. Is your goalie in the right state of mind to get the game going? What is their body language and most importantly what is their inner self-talk. You can help your goalie to remember how SPIN can help put them in the right state of mind. That means a shift in posture, performance breathing, and positive self-talk which in this situation will consist of a performance statement that will help drown out any doubt and install confidence.

Now of course there are going to be times when a quick call will start the game which will have nothing to do with if the goalie is ready to play or not. As a parent what you look for is consistency. Is your son and daughter constantly getting off to a slow start and giving up some quick goals? If it's not consistent, I would advise not to make a big deal about giving up a quick goal and only to reserve the conversation for if it becomes a trend.

3. Play with passion.

If a forward, defenseman or goalie is not having fun while playing there is a problem. Game time should be challenging and there will be ups and downs but at the end of the day, the game should be fun. Once playing hockey becomes a chore or something that a child feels that they have to do it is time to think of doing something else. Passion is such a big part of having success and enjoying what you do. If passion is not there it's going to make it very difficult to move forward in the sport. There is so much in this life to do and so many things to experience, it would be a shame to have someone play hockey just because they feel that they have to. Watch to see if your goalie is playing with the passion of someone that loves the position and loves the game to make sure this is what they want to do. The easiest way to spot passion on the ice is through body language. Sometimes the kids don't talk about their feelings as much as we would hope and it can be difficult for them. Watch out for their body language while they are on the ice in a game like stomping, hanging their shoulders, loosely holding their stick, disinterested in the game, or even apathetic. This is very easy to see from the stands and needs to be addressed if it is an issue. This of course doesn't mean there may be some games that their attention level isn't what'd you expect but we get back to "control what you can control" and the easiest thing to control for a goaltender is their effort. As a goalie parent, you can see the effort in a few different situations such as preparing to stop a shot, trying to stop a rebound or tie up a loose puck, and trying to find the puck in traffic. These situations are signs that a goalie is putting in the effort necessary.

4.   Patience.

At the beginning of this book we took a look at confidence and how confidence was a major key to goaltending. We define confidence as "the ability to act." As you understand watching your goalie one thing that you can look at is whether they are trying to make saves or training not to get scored on. A goalie that plays with confidence is acting and therefore the movement is to stop the puck. A goalie that is trying not to get scored on is hoping the puck hits them and doesn't go in which is the opposite of the ability to act. Therefore, even if you don't know the first thing about the techniques and structures of goaltending, one thing you can look for is how their body is moving towards the puck and going to get it or just staying in place hoping to get hit.

Where the goaltender shows confidence is the ability to wait out shooters. If a goalie goes down early before a shot, the probability of scoring a goal goes in the favor of the shooter. If a goalie goes down early the shooter may opt to pass the puck leaving our goaltender stranded and having to go into desperation to make the save. The goalie that waits out the shooter and is patient will have the best chance to stop the puck. Therefore what you may want to do is pay attention to if a goaltender stays up until the shot is released. Therefore, patience is confidence and confidence is patience. One expression that you will hear coaches use about waiting that extra second is the goalie should "hold their edges". What holding your edges means is to stay on your inside edges which means that the goalie is up and hasn't started going down. You don't have to be an expert to tell whether a youth goalie waits out the shooter or goes down early.

When I was young there was not a lot of coaching for goalies but there was a book that I read by the legendary Jacques Plante called "On Goaltending: Fundamentals of Hockey Netminding by the Master of the Game." I can't tell you how many times I must have read that book. In the end, it had so much useful advice which is still appropriate in today's game. In that book was the first time I read the rule "the goalie should never make the first move." That rule is as applicable today as it was back in the day of Jacques Plante. The easiest situation to think about the rule to never make the first move is on a breakaway. On a breakaway, if the goalie makes the first move on the deke then the shooter may have an open net to put the puck in. As a parent watching the game you can watch if your goalie makes the first move or if they wait out the shooter and then react to what the shooter is going to do.

In today's game finding NHL goalies with patience is not hard to do. Jacques Plante was a goalie for the Montreal Canadiens where there is now a goalie by the name of Carey Price who exemplifies patience. Carey Price plays the game of hockey and the position of a goaltender with such patience and a sense of calm. The calmness in which he plays comes from the experience of playing a lot of hockey games and seeing a lot of different situations and therefore having the confidence to predict what will happen. A calm goalie is going to be able to show more patience than a goalie that plays in a state of panic. If a goalie is all wound up and full of energy it'll be hard to be patient and wait out the shooter. They must be able to control their excitement to read the play and read the release and react to what's going on the ice.

5. Skills.

To play any game or do any job well, a person needs the skills to have success. But what if you are a goalie parent that doesn't know about the proper mechanics that goes into making a save? How can you tell if your goaltender is skillful and has the requisite training to play? One way to identify skill is watching for rebounds. Typically a goaltender that allows a lot of rebounds is lacking the skills necessary to control and dictate where the puck goes after a save. Picture a low shot along the ice right at the goalie... that rebound should be steered out of harm's way and left in a position where the attacking team can't get a second shot. Controlling the puck is a combination of hand-eye coordination and technique. You can also pay particular attention to a shot to the glove. Catching the puck is also a combination of hand-eye coordination and technique. Ideally, the goalie is looking to trap the puck inside the glove and not let the puck drop to the ice for the rebound. If your son or daughter is a good baseball player and catches the ball quite easily in their glove, that should also translate into their ability to catch a puck as a goalie. Therefore, if an athlete has the physical skills to be able to catch this should be the same on the ice. If a goalie is struggling to catch the puck cleanly on the ice it could be a result of a technical issue or a glove break that is not a good fit. We are going to talk more about training and methodology later on in this book.

6. Key saves.

It's funny when you scout hundreds of games how certain things jump out at you. One of the things that I track as a scout while watching goalies is their key saves in a game and typically for a goaltender to win they need to make three key saves in any given game. This is a good number to keep in mind while you're watching your goalie. How many key saves did they make in the game? Now, if you're not a hockey or a goalie expert, how can you determine whether the save was a key save or not? It is pretty easy... when you are watching the game and a play happens where there's a great opportunity for the other team you're instinctually going to know it. I know for myself whenever there is a great opportunity in a game in my head I say the word "GOAL". I know that when I say the word goal in my head and the goalie makes the save that should be marked as a key save.

Key saves can also be related to the game situation and momentum. Therefore a save late in the game with the game on the line can be classified as a key save. Momentum-changing saves can also change the outcome of a game. A momentum-changing save comes when the other team is pushing to score a goal and is carrying the play. A save by the goalie energizes their team and results in a change in momentum, therefore, leading to scoring opportunities and ideally a goal. A key save can also come when the goalie's team is leading... for example, the score is 3-0 and the goalie's team has complete control of the game while the other team is just looking for a crack in the armor to get back in the game. A save that keeps the spread on the score and denies the other team the opportunity to gain momentum is a key save. Recognizing key saves during a game allows for some fun discussion on the way home.

One trick of the trade when it comes to teaching a goalie patience I've learned from the goalie coach of the University of Maine, Alfie Michaud, and it is what he learned from his goalie coach, the legendary Grant Standbrook. What Grant taught goalies back in the day was to say the word "CLICK" right before the release of the shop, therefore causing a fraction of a second delay from going down early and thus increasing patience. Alfie used The Click method in college and in pro which allowed him to play at the highest levels. A great opportunity to practice the Click method for a goalie is to get in the habit of saying click on the release of the shot in practice as it may help them hold their edges longer. Of course, like any suggestions, some goalies will find this very useful while for others it is not the right fit for them.

7. Take the whistle.

Another thing a parent can look for while watching their goalie in the game is to identify whether they can understand the flow of the game. The easiest way to do this is when a goalie has the opportunity to play the puck or to freeze it. Sometimes, when the goalie's team has the momentum it is a better choice to keep the puck moving as opposed to freezing it and therefore keeping the momentum. There are times in the game when the other team is pushing and they are under pressure. It is at that time the goalie needs to do everything they can to stop the play and allow the troops to regroup. Therefore, if a goalie has the opportunity to play the puck or to freeze the puck in this situation they should be freezing the puck and taking the whistle.

There will also be times in the game when freezing the puck is the right choice because the goalie's teammates have been out for a long shift and fresh legs are needed on the ice. When the goalie freezes the puck which results in a face-off, the coach can then send new players on the ice. Freezing the puck may also be a good decision when there is a line mismatch on the ice. What this means is that the other team may have their best players on the ice and the goalie's team has their weakest players trying to keep up. A whistle and a face-off will allow the coach to get the right line match up on the ice and keep the game competitive. A goalie that recognizes a bad matchup and gets a whistle helps avoid a potential goal against. Not only recognizing that teammates are tired or there is a mismatch on the ice, but an experienced goalie can also recognize when they need a break as well and a stoppage of play to reset. A whistle gives a goalie time to rest, grab a drink of water from their water bottle on top of the net and refocus as the play continues.

8. Play the puck.

When I was younger, there was very little goaltending training available. In this day and age, there seems to be a goalie coach around every corner and the level of training has never been better. With so much available on the internet and increased sharing of information, whether it be techniques or strategies, goalie coaches have done a great job elevating the play of goalies around the world. Therefore acquiring goalie training and mastering techniques in the past proved to be a differentiating factor between goalies. The goalie that had obtained training would be able to separate themselves from the pack but that just isn't the case anymore. Goalies have to find other ways if they are going to outdo their competition and one of which is puck handling.

The ability to play the puck for a goaltender is a skill that takes a lot of practice. I would also say that the skill of being able to pass and clear a puck starts at home. There you have the time to practice and all you need is a bucket of pucks and a place to shoot such as a garage or basement. At home, you can structure the shooting in many different ways like the 5,000 puck challenge. The 5,000 puck challenge is a 10-week program where the goalies shoot a hundred pucks a day for 5 days which equals a total of 5000 shots. Doing a program such as the 5,000 puck challenge is a way to make shooting pucks in the basement or the garage more interesting and more fun for the goalies.

The trick about learning how to shoot a puck at home I actually learned from my son Joey. Joey loved to shoot pucks and he was in the basement all the time ripping away. I remember going down frequently and getting upset with him because he was using player gloves and a player stick as opposed to a goalie stick, his goalie blocker, and glove. I told him time and time again that he should be using his blocker and glove if he wanted his shooting practice to translate to the ice. Fortunately, he didn't listen to me and continued to practice with his player gloves and stick. What I didn't realize at the time was that by not having a chunky blocker and glove on along with a heavier goalie stick he was able to learn the mechanics of shooting so his skill of handling the puck improved tremendously. It allowed him to improve the technique better than if he would have been using a blocker and glove. Fast forward to today, it is Joey's puck handling that is a big part of his game and proved to be a differentiating factor as he moved up the ranks.

While watching games, parents can identify if their goalie is playing the puck or not. There is no better chance to learn than actually playing the puck live in games where a goalie must build their confidence doing so. One thing that they are going to have to understand is that the only way to get better at handling the puck is to make mistakes. I would suggest that you encourage your son or daughter to play the puck and you can watch for those opportunities in a game and reinforce positively when they go out to make a play. If they cough one up which results in a goal, make sure that you explain that's just like letting in a goal and letting in goals is the only way that a goalie can get better. Primarily the goal is to get their opportunity to go out of their crease and make a play with the puck on a dump in or a rim. The earlier in their career that they get comfortable leaving the crease to go make a play the better off they will be.

9.   Memory loss.

While watching the game something that a parent can look for is how a goaltender responds after a goal. If you ever watch an NHL game you will notice that almost all goalies do the same thing… a goalie turns around, flips their mask up, and takes a sip of water. Some goalies also go for a skate to the corner of the ice. I believe that all goaltenders should have a routine that they go through following a goal much like the NHL stars that they watch on TV. I recommend right after the puck goes in that the goaltender skates slowly towards the corner and skates back to their net. Once they get back to the net they can grab their water bottle and take a squirt of water. After they have taken a drink of water it is time to get back to the present moment and "SPIN".

SPIN, as we discussed earlier, is about changing your posture, performing a breathing technique, and feeding yourself with positive self-talk. Therefore, after a quick escape to the corner, the goalie can then put his or her chest and shoulders back, hold their head high and take a deep breath in with a long exhale two times, and repeat the mantra of the great Martin Brodeur of never getting beat twice or utter the work "next". Of course, this is the protocol that I teach the goalies and I work with but it may not be what works best for all the goalies. Like any technical strategy, the goaltender has to experiment and find their way and become their own goalie.

A legendary goaltender in Boston is Tim Thomas and I'd like to share a story about him and how it applies to this section. When I was coaching with the Bruins, Tim Thomas was at training camp. He had previously played in Finland after a stellar career at the University of Vermont. Tim had had a tremendous camp but it was time to cut down as it was the last day of training camp. Our general manager was in the coach's office meeting with the players that were getting sent down to our AHL affiliate in Providence, including Tim Thomas. What the general manager didn't realize was that I was going out early on the ice with the goalies and he hadn't met with Tim yet. Before I headed to the ice I walked through the locker room and much to my surprise Tim Thomas was half-dressed with his skates and pads on in his stall preparing to go on the ice. I didn't know what to do because I knew he wasn't supposed to be on the ice and was scheduled to get cut but... was I the one that was going to have to tell him? I walked up to Tim and said good morning and asked him how he was doing. He replied and asked me the same. After I responded, I asked him... "have you checked in with anybody this morning?" He figured out exactly what I was saying and I will never forget his response...he looked me in the eyes and said "if they want to cut me they can drag me off the ice." Tim Thomas was a fierce competitor and an eventual Stanley Cup Champion and it was his competitiveness that was truly his superpower. My response was easy... I simply looked at him and said "okay, let's go." He had his meeting following practice, was cut but rejoined the team two years later and led them to a Stanley Cup.

The reason why I am telling you the story is because Tim Thomas was infamous for his reactions after goals. While we train goaltenders to stay calm and composed after they've been beaten, Tim Thomas was exactly the opposite. Tim would react to a goal as if he was a young goalie getting scored on for the first time. Although it was not exactly what you would want a goaltender to do, it was so pure and genuine that his emotion actually served as an inspiration to the team. He is one of the few goalies that I've ever seen that could pull this off. For me it is the opposite of what we try to teach but a good example that not everyone fits in the same box. Watching how your goaltender responds to goals is something that every parent can do and at the right time discuss with their goalie how they want to act. It would be ideal to put a system in place for how they will respond each time they get scored on.

The key is the ability for the goaltender to have that short memory and move on to the next shot. Another analogy that you can use with your goalie is that of driving a car but not looking through the rear-view mirror. The point of the analogy is that if you look through the rear-view mirror you are looking behind you and not looking forward. On the ice with the play about to continue is not the time that a goaltender should be thinking about what just happened but more importantly what will happen next. An elite goaltender that can refocus and not let one goal turn into three. If warranted there is plenty of time after the game to analyze a goal against and to plan what to do the next time that shot occurs but during the game it is essential to stay in the moment and simply move on.

As a parent, we recognize that playing sports is a microcosm of life and therefore the way they conduct themselves on the ice, on the court or in the field is an example of the type of person that they are. There's a great expression that goes... Sports does not develop character, it exposes character. As parents, we can watch games and be able to spot tendencies and habits. All of our kids have the opportunity to be able to use these examples as teaching moments.

One thing that I've always been proud of watching my kids is some of the simple things that would make any parent proud. Both Joey and Alex following each game would go up to the referees for a quick thank you. I looked forward to the end of each game because regardless of the outcome it proved to me that playing the game was creating some lasting positive life habits. Thanking the referees while leaving the ice as well as the coaches when exiting the locker room are simple demonstrations of respect that were repeated time and time. It is the repetition that creates good habits and solidifies their character as they move on through life.

As a hockey rink owner, I'm very proud of the facilities that we offer our goalies and have a great amount of appreciation for the kids that show respect to the facility by cleaning up after themselves. Making sure that the kids understand that playing the great sport of hockey is not a right but a privilege is something that we can all teach. Hockey players and goalies should be respectful of the facilities that they play in and make sure they throw away the trash, pick up after themselves and be cognizant of the language that they use. Especially during the formative years as the kids start to expand their vocabulary, it will fill parents with pride.

10. Keeping stats and taking videos.

As technology continues to improve at an exponential rate it is more available for parents to use to track on-ice performance. There are simple apps that can easily act as a shot counter for goalies and there are more advanced apps that allow for parents to track a wide variety of metrics from the game. I have read articles that have discouraged parents from using apps during the game. I think the choice of whether to use an app to record statistics or a phone camera to video the game is up to the parent and a lot of it has to do with the child and what they like but both can be beneficial.

I think that video is a great way for goalies to learn. If a parent is going to either use their phone or a video camera to record the game I would suggest not trying to be like an NHL cameraman and follow the play up and down the ice while zooming in and out. What I believe works best is that when the play enters the goalie's zone to hit the record button and stay on until the puck exits the zone. The phone or camera should be held stationary and fixed on the goalie. What you should be able to see in the frame should be from the top of the circles to the boards behind the net. What this provides is that there is enough of the action so you can see how the goalie is reading the play but is also close enough to see the mechanics. When reviewing the game now the goalie is only watching clips of him or her playing as opposed to watching the full game. This will make it much quicker for the goalie to watch themselves and can prove to be an extremely valuable tool. When I played as a youth, I never had a chance to see what I looked like in net and wished that I would have had the opportunity to see myself and how I looked as compared to how I thought I looked.

Some parents recognize that videotaping games are valuable. I don't think parents have to video every game but I do think it's important that every once in a while you pull out the phone and get some video of your son or daughter between the pipes. If you are self-conscious about this and worried about being labeled the overbearing hockey parent you can pick rinks where you would not stand out as much while recording. One aspect of recording that is overlooked is that for the parent that gets nervous during games it gives them something to do. Much like I found it easier to watch as a coach because I was occupied throughout the game. Recording can have the same effect and make it easier for the parent. I think that recording has become much more common and can provide not only video as a learning tool but as a goaltender gets older it can be used as a recruiting tool as well.

When it comes to using goalie apps, there is a number to choose from. I recently released an app called SIG Game Day. The reason I created an app was because of the frustration that I was experiencing with coaches interpreting a goalie's performance. As a goalie coach, you enter the coach's room in between each period and after the game and are often questioned by the coaches about certain goals or situations that involve the goaltender. The goalie coach is often put in a position where they have to defend their goalie and the conversation is not much different from a he-said-she-said argument.

What happens for a coach is that they have so much to watch in a game and when it comes to the goaltender they are often watching what I frame as short clips as opposed to the whole videos. They will see something, make a mental video clip, and that then becomes what they remember of the game. Therefore, a goalie can do a great job on their rebounds but if the coach makes a mental video clip of one that got away, in their opinion the goalie did not do a good job controlling the rebounds. As a goalie coach defends their goalie it then becomes their opinion versus the coach's opinion. SIG Game Day was developed to be an objective tool used to evaluate the performance of goalies with no subjectivity involved.

When it comes to evaluating a goalie's performance I use the same four metrics all the time. They are 1. Goal Expectancy. 2. Rebound Control, 3. Glove Performance and 4. Playmaking. What SIG Game Day does objectively is track these four keys during the game and is designed so that parents and coaches can use the tool intuitively so that they can put information in real-time and keep their eyes on the play as much as possible. By recording these statistics as the game goes on parents and coaches have a real-time picture of the goaltender's performance free of any bias. The statistics can de-escalate any conflict that may come when there are two opposing views. This provides the coach, goalie coach, parent, and goaltender the means to evaluate their game and the key elements are strictly at a statistical level as opposed to listening to someone express their opinion or interpretation.

SIG Game Day can be used on a tablet or a phone. Parents and coaches using the app simply tap on the screen each time there's a shot and thus classifying what type of shot it was. Each shot has a probability or expectancy of going in the net and resulting in a goal. By tracking goal expectancy, the playing field for goalies is leveled because it allows the goalie that plays for a weaker team to be evaluated based on the probability of shots that they are facing and not have the benefit of having great stats because they do not face many high danger shots.

Rebound control is also tracked objectively. A green rebound button is tapped if there is a shot on the net and the goaltender makes the save and the rebound ends up in possession of the goalie's team. If the opposing team gets possession of the rebound a red rebound button is tapped and if the goalie freezes the puck and there is no rebound, a black button is tapped. Therefore rebound control analysis is no longer if the goalie steers the puck to the corner of the rink but is evaluated by who gets control of the puck. By analyzing rebound control in this fashion there is no subjectivity to rebound control and it becomes an objective stat, free of opinion. Just in case you're curious, a good rebound control or as I like to refer to it as rebound retention is 66%. A good freeze rate or no rebound rate is 33% or better.

SIG Game Day also tracks glove performance. When a shot is taken at the glove the green glove button is tapped if the goalie makes a save. If the puck beats the goalie to the glove it is recorded in red. If the goalie cleanly catches the puck the black glove button is tapped. By recording the shot to the glove the coach then has statistical proof of how good the glove skills of a goalie are? Therefore, if a goalie gets beat one goal to the glove the coach then isn't saying that the goalie's glove hand isn't good enough. The coach can then look at the number of shots that are taken to the glove side and how many are stopped and how many are frozen. This is a more accurate way to analyze a goalie's glove skill as opposed to having one video clip in the mind of a coach and therefore suggesting that the goalie's glove hand is an issue. At the same time, it is interesting to see how many pucks that are shot to the glove are cleanly caught versus just being stopped. This is an interesting metric to see as it is a reflection of the skill level of the goaltender.

Some people will advise you not to keep stats and to chart the game and I can completely understand where it's coming from. They intend that the goaltender focuses on their performance, particularly their effort, and compete regardless of the outcome and that stats are based on the individual and not the team and it can be a distraction. I think the stats for a goaltender, particularly in the SIG Game Day, can prove to be a valuable learning tool that should be used to help the individual goalie and not as comparable to the other goalies.

Andrew Raycroft played 11 seasons in the NHL and won the Rookie of the Year award with the Boston Bruins in 2003. He also played for the Toronto Maple Leafs, the Colorado Avalanche, and the Dallas Stars. If you ask Andrew about what it means to play across the ice against the other goaltender he would tell you that the other goalie had no impact on how he played. His outlook of playing goalie was similar to that of a golfer. He said a golfer plays against himself because his score is not impacted by the person that they are playing with. It is the golfer versus the course. Andrew Raycroft feels that goaltending is similar to that of a golfer because as opposed to playing the golf course the goalie is playing the other team. Figuring out how to beat the other team is similar to how a golfer approaches how they will play a particular course. How this applies to stats is that stats help a goaltender assess how they play and where there needs to be an improvement.

Post Game

After the game is over the parents' role is still vital concerning the experience of being a goalie. The way that a parent interacts with their son or daughter after a game can either improve the experience of playing hockey and being a goalie or take away from it. Therefore, having a routine of how things are handled after the game is important to have. From where to meet up and how to discuss the game, the post-game may either fuel the passion or be an energy vampire.

My two sons are opposites as people and therefore I had a different routine for both of them. Joey was outgoing and very social and he would like nothing better than to hang with the boys in the locker room as long as he could or play around in the lobby of the rink. He was what you would call a rink rat and would like nothing more than to hang out and spend time around the rink. My other son Alex was much quieter, was not a social butterfly or a rink rat, and shortly after the game was ready to go home.

With that being said, when Joey was younger I took my time leaving the rink so that he could hang with his buddies and watch some of the next game. To this day Joey still "lives" at the hockey rink. Alex on the other hand was out of the locker room quickly and ready to go. He was not as curious about watching the next game on the ice or chatting up his teammates. It just wasn't his personality at that time but fast forward to College and he has become more social and enjoys hanging out in the locker room and the rink. In this section, I will offer some advice on how the post-game experience of a goalie can be handled by their parents.

1. Where to?

Once the game is over there is a new routine that takes place and that routine is where you are going to meet up with your son or daughter. With younger kids, you may be in the locker room helping them get changed. At a certain point, there will come a time where a parent entering the locker room is not appropriate anymore. No one will have to tell you when this time comes as it will be apparent. Once a goalie is old enough to be on their own in the locker room then it's going to be a matter of where to meet them afterward. I think it's important for them to know what to expect when they leave that locker room and meet up with their parents. When you're dropping off you can simply let them know where you were going to meet up.

While waiting for a son or daughter you may be interacting with the other parents. It is important that you interact socially with the other parents in the same way regardless of whether the game is won or lost. Some parents prefer to wait in the car for older kids so that they can make a phone call or two while they are waiting. If this is the case then once again it should be consistent. If a parent does not wait around for the kids with the other parents, sometimes it could be misread as anti-social, especially to a group of close-knit parents. Just keep that in mind while you are in the rink and interacting if you are a parent that goes to the car immediately after the game. If you are going to be in the car just remember to let your son and daughter know where to go after the game.

2.   Carry their bag.

I can remember when I was playing hockey in high school back in Montreal. I lived on the West Island and would have to take the train each day to Loyola High School. I lived about a mile from the train station and would walk each day. I can clearly remember the days I had to walk to the train station with my hockey bag and sticks along with my backpack for school. I'm not going to lie, that was not fun, but it was the price that I had to pay if I wanted to play for the high school team. You wanted to make the varsity team because we had our locker room so I wouldn't have to carry my equipment back and forth to the train. I think it's important that the goal is to carry their bag and I know even though it's heavy it is something that at a certain age that the parents have to leave it to their child.

As soon as the goalie is strong enough to carry their bag they should. A lot of goalies have a bag just for their equipment and leave their pads outside the bag. Therefore, along with their hockey gear, they have their pads and their sticks. I think it's cool to see a parent walking in with their goalie carrying either the sticks or the pads while the goalie is carrying their bag. And with so many bags having wheels on them now it is also becoming a lot easier for younger goalies to be responsible for their gear. As you're going to read about in the clear section of this book, the equipment is sometimes a big part of the allure of becoming a goaltender in the first place.

Car Coaching

At the beginning of this book, one of the sections you read was about don't listen to players' parents because the life of a goalie is much different from the life of a player. Most youth hockey associations will tell parents that they should just be parents and not car coach their children. They will tell you that it is a coach's responsibility to teach the kids how to play hockey and that our parents' influence can sometimes be detrimental to what the coach is trying to do. For me, this does not apply to goalie parents. Typically a goalie is not getting coached like the other players and I like to refer to goaltending as a sport in itself.

Think about what a different experience a goalie has when they play a game as opposed to being on the bench and interacting with the players. Players in between shifts are getting instruction by the coaches throughout the game. While this is going on, the goalie is basically on an island as he or she stands in their crease with no interaction with the coaches. The only time that a goalie may communicate with a coach during a game is in between periods and this isn't always the case. Sometimes, the younger goalies will simply skate from one end to the other, and going to the bench doesn't necessarily mean that they will be talking to a coach. Sometimes the coach just gets all the kids together and gives them some team instructions or a pep talk.

It is not much different when the game ends. The goalie returns to the locker room to listen to the coach addressing the team about their performance but in all likelihood will receive little to no coaching on anything specific to them and their position. You can argue that it is better this way because most coaches are not knowledgeable about how to play goalie and do not want to address their goaltenders because they don't want to... mess them up. Therefore, it is more common than not that the goalie has very little interaction with any of the coaches. If you do have a coach that is responsible for the goaltenders and communicates with them, then you can count yourself as one of the lucky ones.

Because of the lack of interaction goaltenders typically receive pre, during and post-game, car coaching is encouraged in the goalie world. There are parents who have taken it upon themselves to learn as much as they can about the position of goaltending so they could help their children more because they get frustrated. By no means would I ever expect a parent to study goaltending to coach their son or daughter. But there are so many things that a parent can do to help their child without knowing the techniques and strategies of the position. It is these little things that can be discussed in the car that can dramatically impact whether the goalie is having a positive experience or a negative one. Therefore, car coaching becomes a big part of the goalie's development, and hopefully, through my years of experience as a goalie and parent, I can offer a few tips about car coaching that will help you out with your kids as well.

As I mentioned earlier in this section, my kids have two completely different personalities. My older son Joey hopped in the car as a youngster and was full of energy regardless of the score. I would always chuckle at how he started talking about the game. Joey's team may have lost 6-0 and he could have faced only 20 shots but he would look at me wide-eyed with a big smile and the first thing he would say would be, "Dad, did you see that glove save I made in the third period". It would always crack me up how he could get lit up but still be excited about making a big glove save. I knew that he was a kid that had a good perspective on the game and that I didn't have to worry about too much.

My younger son Alex was the total opposite. Alex's team would lose a game 1-0 and he would make 30 saves but the first thing that came out of his mouth was… "What a terrible goal I gave up. I can't believe I cost the team the game". It simply amazes me how we can frame and interpret things in any way we want. Joey could come out of the game where he didn't play as well as he could have and still enjoy the experience of making a big save. Alex could play a terrific game but still, be hard on himself despite the fact his team should have lost by two or three goals. This being said, there is no one way to interact with our kids that applies to everyone. Knowing how to communicate after a game starts with knowing your child and how they process things. Having a strategy on how to approach your goalie after games will be based on their personality and their character and your success will come with learning to navigate how best to communicate.

1. Communication.

Communication after the game in the car is important because I think it helps in the long run for a goaltender not to internalize the events of the game if they were negative. I remember how helpful it was to me to be able to discuss goals with my father after the game. It allowed me to talk it through and understand what happened and therefore be able to prepare for the next one. If you don't talk it through then the negative feeling of a shot that should have stopped can sometimes weigh on a goalie and just sit there. As a coach, the practice after a game, I like to do is what I like to call a cleanse and for me what a cleanse is means getting on the ice the next practice and replicating exactly what happened leading up to the goal and the shot. This exercise allows the goalie to have another chance at stopping the puck and do it repeatedly with success so that they feel confident that they will be able to make the save the next time and therefore they can replace the negative emotion of that goal with a positive one.

2. Batter Up.

In my opinion when the kids see their parents after the initial part of the interaction I think it is important that the interaction should be the same whether their team won or lost the game or how they played. I tried to be consistent in my approach each time as my goal was to let my kids know that I was there to support them regardless of the outcome and that I was proud of them for getting out on the ice to compete. I also didn't want them to think that if they lost the game or didn't play well that I was disappointed in them as a person or overemphasize the importance of a win or a loss, particularly at the younger levels. Therefore, I tried to greet my kids with a smile each and every time which was typically followed by a tap of the knuckles or a hug.

I was always very conscious, particularly if there were any other parents or players in the area, to never comment about their play in front of anyone. I think the last thing that a kid wants to hear is their parents teasing them about their play in front of other people. Any comment that I would make initially would be strictly related to the team and not any individual. In that same vein, I would also strictly stay away from saying anything about the other team or anybody on their team. The last thing that I would want to project is that of someone that complains. My interactions with my kids were always consistent and positive to put the game in perspective which in turn I hoped would lead to a positive discussion.

3. The Lead.

After we got in the car, I always knew that Joey was going to speak first and I knew that I was the one that was going to have to start the conversation with Alex. It is only normal for both the kids and the parents to want to discuss the goals, how they went in, and if there was a better way to play them. Starting the conversation for me should not begin with the goals against but rather the team's outcome. It is so important for a goalie to realize that they are one cog in the wheel and a goalie's role is to do whatever they can to help the team win and that a goal is a reflection of much more than just the goalie. If we focus on the team and what's best for the team it then can reduce the emphasis on individual achievement and stats. By discussing the team it is an easier way to start the conversation and gets the communication flowing.

4. What a save.

After discussing how the team did as a whole and how the game went, the conversation can progress to the goalie's performance. The goal of this part of the conversation is to start talking about the good saves as opposed to anything that may have happened negatively in the game such as a goal against. Somehow we spend so much time dissecting the goals as opposed to looking at all the positive aspects of making a save. Talking about the good habits that went into making those saves hopefully will translate to more saves just like them.

Once again a parent does not have to know about the mechanics or the strategy that went into making a safe. The goalie needs to know that you saw the big save and your excitement about them making the safe will have an impact on the game. You can ask questions such as… "How did the play happen? Did you see it all the way? Did you think you were going to stop it?" Let your son or daughter explain what they saw and you can simply ask questions, it will allow them to talk and explain to you what happened out on the ice as opposed to you telling them what they should or should not have done.

5. The goals against.

After you've had a chance to discuss how the team did and some of the key saves it's time to talk about the goals against. For me, the main outcome of this discussion is that I'm looking for a way to give my goalie the chance to talk it through and put it to bed. Once again my approach would be to simply ask questions about the goal and let them do the talking. As I noted earlier the only way a goalie is going to get better is to get beat. Therefore, there's nothing negative about the goals because the only thing that can come out of goals against is a knowledge of how to stop them in the future. In discussing the goals against the parent's role is simply to listen and ask questions.

One thing important for goalies is to be accountable for the goals against. By listening you can get a feeling for whether your son or daughter is accepting that responsibility. You may find that they are frequently blaming their teammates, coaches, and bad luck. The real focus should be on what they could have done to prevent the goal. One strategy that I use for this is to grade the goals against them. I classify goals in four different ways… 1. No Chance, 2. Could Have, 3. Should Have and 4. Weak. You'll get a good idea of the accountability factor. What you are going to find is that most goals will fall under the number two category of Could-Have. If you ask your son or daughter to grade the goals, the question that should follow is simple… "What do you think you could have done differently to prevent the goal"? The same applies to if the response was number three or four. The focus should be on what the goalie could have done and not on the teammate or the coach. By all means, do I recognize the fact that it could very well have been a poor defensive play that resulted in the goal, and quite possibly the defensive structure of the team may not be the best? By blaming the others the result will be a lack of accountability by the goalie and will not help them concerning their mindset moving forward. Once again I think it's important to know that your role is not to teach technique or strategy, but rather to listen to what your goalie has to say and allow them to talk it through.

6. Figure it out.

Being a good goaltender is simply having the ability to figure out how to make a save. Also having strong mechanics and structure help but some goalies are lacking those skills and can still stop the puck. Parents when talking to their kids about goaltending as well as the game shouldn't feel that it's up to them to explain what their child should have or should not have done. Figuring it out is a big part of the development of a goaltender.

John Vanbiesbrouck is a legend in USA Hockey and before Jonathan Quick was the most winning US-born goalie in the history of the NHL. If you speak with John, he will tell you the key to developing a goaltender is putting them in a situation where they face the most adversity possible. If they can survive and conquer then they will be a goalie. John himself left his home in Michigan to play Junior Hockey in Canada in Sault Ste. Marie. He was an undersized American goalie trying to make it in Canada's game in their own backyard... and he did just that.

John is a big proponent of having goalies figure it out. He considers it a detriment when goalie coaches have to explain every aspect of every situation of every goal to the goalies. Parents can learn from John and his approach as he wants the goaltender to figure out what they should have done and what they need to do the next time to succeed. This puts accountability and maturity on the shoulders of the goaltender and they learn to fend for themselves and figure out how to take the test without someone providing the answers for them.

7. Keep it real.

One of the things that my wife Daniela and I feel strongly about is keeping it real with our kids. It is what it is and our approach has always been to be honest about things and not try to paint a prettier picture of a situation.

When it came to talking about hockey we did the same thing with them. Although we've always felt that we were supportive of Joey and Alex we would never try to simply cover over when they didn't play well or over emphasize when they had a great game. We tried to keep it real and honest with them when we were discussing their performance. We felt that treating them like two adults at an early age concerning the way that we discussed events with them would help in their maturation as people.

As a coach, I give a lot of advice to kids and try to teach them lessons both on the ice and off the ice. One of the things that I'm cognizant of is that when I do praise a goaltender for doing something well that those praises do not go unnoticed because there is so much of it that it is just blended in with everything else that I say. I would not say that as a coach I am hard on the goalies but I would say that I work hard at keeping it real. When I am out on the ice with the goalies and they are not doing something well I tell them and try to teach them how to do it better. By pointing out when they do things wrong and not just simply praising them for every time they do something right I believe that when I do praise them it means more. I strongly believe that by being honest and straightforward as a coach when it comes time to give accolades they become a much more powerful tool as opposed to being drowned in them. As a parent, I take the same approach and simply try to keep it real.

8. Highs and Lows.

I remember having a conversation with an NHL Scout and former NCAA National Championship coach Mike Addesa early on in my coaching career. I can vividly remember sitting in my living room and having this conversation and the advice that Mike gave me. He told me that I was just getting going and the most important thing to learn is not to get too high or too low as a coach. Although this falls in the category of easier said than done it was great advice which I give to all young coaches myself. As a coach, you are so invested in the kids and want so much for them to do well that you get excited with the wins and so disappointed with the losses. Mike encouraged me to stay even keel and not to let my emotions get the best of me. It was some of the best advice I've ever received and also applies to goalies.

I would like to hand that same advice over to goalie parents. All we want as parents is for our kids to be happy. We have so much love for our kids and watching them grow is an emotional journey. We feel proud of our kids when they graduate, receive an award, or get a job ...etc. These are exciting times and times to celebrate. We also feel their pain when they suffer adversity such as getting a bad grade, getting cut from a team, losing a job... etc. The thing about watching our kids play sports is that it's an instantaneous success or failure right before our eyes when a goalie makes a big save or gives a goal. A parent that can stay calm and not overdue a big win or a big loss and simply support their goaltender is providing exactly what the goalie needs.

In my opinion, there is one question above all following a game that is the most important question to be asked... "Did you have fun?" Look, at the end of the day, if your kids aren't having fun playing hockey there's a problem. If a goalie is not enjoying the game as much as others may need a shift in perspective. Maybe he or she is either putting too much pressure on themselves and trying too hard or not trying hard enough because they do not want to put themselves out there. The perspective of the game is what is going to allow goalies the enjoyment regardless of the outcome. Of course, it is a lot more fun to win a game but that should not be the only fun that is derived from hockey. There's so much that can be learned and enjoyed besides just the wins or the losses at the end of the game. If the answer to the question "Did you have fun?" is a negative one it will warrant further discussion. If it is a positive one after the game then it is going to fill the goalie with passion and fuel future success and enjoyment.

Above all, at the end of the day, a parents' role is to be supportive and provide opportunities for their kids. By allowing your kids to play hockey and sacrificing your time and finances you're allowing them to play a sport they love. Your obligation isn't to become a goalie coach and tell them exactly what they should be doing at all times. A parent's role is simply to support, encourage and be there for their child to help them figure it out. If you can do that as a parent you would have been able to provide exactly what your child needs from you, the rest is up to them.

9. Unpack and it's over.

Once you get back home after the game the first thing a goaltender should be doing is to unpack their bag. Being responsible and taking care of their equipment is an important life skill that young athletes can learn and will help them throughout their life. It is not a parent's responsibility to unpack their kid's hockey equipment and it is solely up to them. It is part of paying the price to be able to get to do something that you want to do. Therefore, not only is it a sanitary and important way to maintain equipment but it is also part of character development and maturation.

There is also a symbolic aspect to emptying the bag and having the equipment put away so it can dry and be ready for the next game. Once the equipment is put away after the game it should be over. Look, you've already discussed the game in the car. You've been supportive of your goalie and allowed him or her to talk out the events of the game. After the equipment has been put away it is also time to put that game to bed and to move on…

"Next". This is especially true when it comes to a game that didn't go as well as hoped. You don't want your goaltender to carry around any baggage throughout the day because a sporting event didn't go as well as they hoped. Emptying the bag is symbolic of moving on and not looking through the rear-view mirror. If at a young age you can teach your goaltender to turn the corner and create the habit of emptying their bag and turning the page from the game it will be a great lesson learned.

Goalie Parent Interview #4: Cindy Driedger

Chris Driedger, a 1994 born goalie, was originally selected in the third round of the 2012 NHL draft by the Ottawa Senators and played the 2020-2021 season with the Florida Panthers, leading them to the NHL playoffs and losing to eventual Stanley Cup Champions the Tampa Bay Lightning. Born and raised in Manitoba, Canada, he played for the Winnipeg Monarchs and earned his way to the CHL and the Western Hockey League where in 2014 he became the Calgary Hitmen's all-time saves leader and was selected to the CHL/NHL Prospects Game. After five seasons with the Senators organization, he became a full-time NHL'er with the Panthers.

When did your son decide to be a goalie?

It was actually Chris's younger brother that was the big hockey enthusiast in our family. We weren't a hockey family or fans but because of his brother, we had both kids play. Chris was 7 years old when he started and at that age, the teams are required to rotate players so that everybody gets a chance as a goalie. In his first game, his team won 15 nothing and he was so bored he skated to the bench in the middle of the second period while the play was still going on to tell the coaches that he wasn't getting any shots! The second game he played he saw more action and after the game, the coach recommended that he play on a summer tournament team in what's called the Super Seven. From that point forward he became a goalie.

What did you feel about that decision?

We have always been supportive of whatever activities either of our boys wanted to try, so if he wanted to be a goalie in hockey, which was fine with us. Chris is fortunate to be a very good athlete and is able to adapt and learn how to play different sports quickly. He was already a big kid at his age and he just took to being a goalie. We knew very little about being hockey parents but we figured it out as we went along.

What has been the best part of the journey so far?

As parents what we really enjoy about our boys playing hockey is the hockey community itself. Even now in the NHL, it is great to be part of that community. Hockey parents have a bond forged by sitting for hours in cold rinks and other aspects of hockey practices and games. Goalie parents bond even more because of the uniqueness of their son or daughter's position. There are so many intricacies of playing goalie. The fascinating thing about being a goalie parent is it doesn't matter how old or what level they play at there's a bond amongst us all.

What has been the most challenging part of being a goalie parent?

The toughest part about being a goaltender's parent is to understand that a goal is the team's failure, to which the goalie may or may not have contributed. In order for a puck to cross the goal line typically several mistakes have been made before the puck even gets to the goaltender. Once you realize as a parent that a goal is the team's to own, you will find it much less stressful to see goals being scored and appreciate all the good plays the team makes. Keeping in mind that goaltending is 90% mental, it's important to keep positive when you talk to your goalie about any goal. It took us a while to figure this out, so don't despair if it takes you as new goalie parents some time before you're able to talk about goals without making your goalie feel like it's all on them. For our son, we learned to ask " So what happened on that goal?"

What were the key aspects of his development that stand out to you?

One thing that I learned is that there's a transition period from player to goalie skates. Players' skates have a rocker while goalie skates are more or less flat so skating is significantly different. The first time we put Chris in goalie skates was at a practice and he was embarrassed because he kept falling down. One of the best things we did was put Chris in power skating lessons with his goalie skates on and to this day skating is one of his better attributes. My suggestion to goalie parents is to allow their kids to practice using their goalie skates on their own such as public skating or the pond as opposed to putting them on the ice with the other kids and then struggling to get a handle on it. After they get comfortable on their goalie skates then it is time to use their goalie skates for practices and games.

Do you get nervous watching games and if so how do you combat those nerves?

I don't typically get nervous. I don't mind if the team wins or loses, that's hockey. There have been a few games when I've had to leave the room, usually when the reffing is very lopsided and players are in danger of being hurt. I'm not overly concerned about Chris being injured because the goalie wears the most protective equipment on the ice. I'm actually more comfortable with him being a goalie than if he was a player constantly getting checked and at risk of concussion.

What is one piece of advice you would give other goalie parents?

The best advice I could give to other goalie parents is to enjoy the journey. The game is supposed to be fun and if you're not having fun watching your child having fun then there is an issue. Enjoy your son or daughter enjoying playing the game as opposed to worrying about the outcome. I think a parent should help take away the pressure of being a goalie because it's not about being the best as there are always going to be goalies that are better. It's about going out and doing your best and enjoying playing the game. Even to this day, I love watching post-game interviews when Chris talks about the game and says "that was such a fun game to play in."

Training

For the last 25 years I have been training goaltenders and I can't believe how far that training has come. When I was just starting there was a new product called synthetic ice that a lot of players worked on for their shot with their skates on and goalies to practice their technique as well. I started doing private one-on-one lessons with goalies back in 1999. At that time for a goalie to get individualized instruction in a one-on-one format was a rarity. I started with about 10 clients in a small synthetic ice room in Salem, New Hampshire. Now fast forward to 2021 where my company trains over 1,000 goalies annually, mostly in our Development Centers spread throughout Massachusetts on real ice surfaces. Starting with 1 on 1 private lessons where I was creating the curriculum, each and every lesson has now morphed into a system that helps goaltenders get the personalized training they need at a price point that allows families to provide the goalie training without breaking the bank.

As a young goalie coach, I started to experiment with the difference between one-on-one lessons, two goalies and one coach, three goalies and one coach plus one shooter, two goalies with one coach and two shooters…basically, I tried it all! It took years to get to the system of four goalies with two nets, one coach and two shooters; it is this formula that ended up to be magic. A big part of the magic formula is the energy of having four like-minded motivated athletes on the ice at the same time. Not only do the goalies feed off each other but as a coach you feed off the energy in the room and it makes the sessions more dynamic and enjoyable. With four goalies on the ice, there are two goalies in net and two goalies watching an iPad replay of when they were in net while resting for their next shift. This allows the coach to work with both goalies in net at the same time while the shooters put the pucks exactly where the coach needs them to go. The shooters become part of the magic because they understand the timing and placement necessary for the goalies to get the shots.

A lot of people feel that one-on-one private lessons are the best way for athletes to learn and hone their skills and although I agree that private lessons are a great tool I realized that the key to learning for a goaltender was based on repetition and muscle memory. If private lessons were going to be the environment that goalies were going to learn in, most families would not have the means to provide the number of lessons necessary to teach the body how to move correctly and consistently. Putting goaltenders on the ice at the same time decreases the cost for each goaltender and allows for the blend of personal instruction in an energized environment at the right price point for most. The small group lessons became the best way that I could provide training for goalies and countless motivated goaltenders benefited from this type of training.

Small group lessons have allowed me to fine-tune a curriculum over my 25 years in the business and through trial and error, I learned how goalies best develop. In this section, I will talk about training and offer advice to parents on what I have found to be most successful. Like anything in this book, there is not a one-size-fits-all approach to training as we all know that kids learn differently. Hopefully, you'll be able to use some of my experience to help craft a training plan for your son or daughter.

1. Training vs. Practice.

One thing that's important for all parents to understand is there's a major difference between training and practice for a goaltender. Training consists of goalie-specific drills and exercises specifically designed for the position of a goaltender. Practice is what a goalie participates in with their team and is a vehicle in which to practice what they've learned in training. Because practice is designed for a team that includes forwards, defensemen and goalies, what a goalie is going to need is to develop their particular skill set for their position and this is not going to be able to be taught in a practice environment. Parents can't expect that their son or daughter is going to get what they need out of practice without combining practice with training. Training is something goalie parents often have to seek outside of the organization or the team that the goalie plays for. Some goalies are fortunate to have organizations that provide the netminders training but often it is up to the goalie's families to seek out training opportunities separate from their youth hockey organizations.

Goalie coaches will tell you that there is a constant battle between goalie-coaches and player-coaches on how the drills would be best suited for the team and the goaltender. Although, it has come a long way from back when I played, there is so much room for improvement. A lot of times the drills are designed for rapid shots which won't allow the goaltender to track rebounds and get set for the next shot. There's also a lot of discussion and studies revolving around the overuse of blocking techniques and the impact on the goalie's hip health. As you read in the practice section there are ways that goalies can practice and protect themselves from overuse and injuries.

talk to Will about 10-20

2. Don't listen... again.

When it comes to goaltending training a goalie parent should be wary of the advice given by player parents. Forwards and defensemen have specific needs and physical training is different from what the goaltender needs. Player training is much different from a goaltender. All you have to do is look at a player clinic and you will notice the difference. Player clinics can be held with as little as one coach per 12 skaters and there is no way to be able to provide adequate goalie training with the same coach to player ratio. The manner in which goaltending mechanics and structure are taught is different between a goalie and their goalie coach than that of a player and player-coach.

3. Mechanics and Structure.

Every coach uses their own terminology and by no means am I any different. Two of the words that I use quite frequently are mechanics and structure and mechanics for me, are the movements the goalie makes while making a save. Think about a butterfly and how the knees drop to the ice, the positioning of the elbows and gloves, and how the head moves to track the puck into the body. A goalie with strong mechanics is a goalie whose body moves fluidly with the economy and motion when making saves. I will also sometimes use the word technique, in the same manner, I use the word strategy in the same vein as structure. When you are using the word structure my emphasis is how the goalie plays the position. Therefore, a goalie with good structure stays between the pipes and does not chase the play, and has an understanding of how they want to play each situation. So let's take a look at a 3 on 1 offensive zone rush. The puck carrier enters the zone down the wing and the goalie addresses the play and adjusts his or her positioning based on the movement of the puck carrier. In this case, we're going to imagine the puck carrier driving down the boards and making a drop pass to a trailer. How the goalie follows the play and then gaps out on the drop pass to improve their net coverage is their structure. After the trailer takes the shot and the goalie makes a save... that is the mechanics. Hopefully, you can see how mechanics and structure mean two different things, and moving forward you will have a good understanding when I use these two terms.

Goalies need to work on both their mechanics and structure. Teaching the body how to move correctly early on in a goalie's career will pay dividends throughout the length of the time. To train mechanics, the key is repetition and making the same save over and over using proper form. Training mechanics is extremely difficult to do in practice because of the unpredictability of shots in that their placement is random. The structure is when a goaltender is working on drills that require them to position themselves correctly based on the situation that they are facing. A strong goaltending program will incorporate drills that teach both mechanics and structure.

4.   Swipe right.

As a parent you're looking for the best training for your son or daughter and that means finding the right goalie coach. Finding that coach will be a big part of whether a goaltender will be able to progress from season to season. Going back 10 or 20 years there was a big discrepancy between goalie coaches that understood progressive techniques and the best way to play and the goalie coaches that were teaching old school philosophy and methods. Because of a boom in the number of goalie coaches and the ability to stay current with technique and strategy through social media, the difference between what is being taught in the different goalie schools is not nearly as great as it has been in the past.

A few years ago at our annual symposium former Boston Bruins goaltender Andrew Raycroft did a presentation to a roomful of goalie coaches. His presentation was a review of all the goaltending coaches he has had throughout his career which was quite fascinating. He spoke of goalie coaches that were very strong in teaching mechanics while others were excellent with teaching structure. Some of the coaches he had were very good communicators as well as providing him the support that he needed. The most important part of his presentation that struck a chord with all the coaches in attendance was that Andrew didn't feel that the ability to teach mechanics and structure or to be able to communicate well or run great drills was the key to goalie coaching. He said that for him knowing that the goalie coach was there to help and was not simply there for themselves was the key. So, therefore, it didn't matter what aspect of teaching the goalie coach was doing as long as the goalie felt that it was first about the person and goalie position second, the relationship was going to be a strong one and much was going to be accomplished.

Like in any relationship some people get along better with some than others. For a goaltender, building a bond with their goalie coach is extremely important because most goalies stick with their goalie coach for a long time. Unlike players who attend a number of different camps run by different coaches and companies, a goaltender traditionally sticks with one coach or company throughout the majority of their development years. Finding a coach or company that fits your goalie may take some time but eventually, I am sure you're going to find the right place.

5. Batting cage.

When I was younger I loved playing baseball. I had to choose at one point whether to pursue college baseball or hockey. Being from the Province of Quebec you would think the question would have been easier than it was. I had the opportunity to play for the provincial team in the summers while in high school and the program was developed by Major League Baseball to increase the amount of Canadians playing in MLB. I ended up choosing to play hockey and I couldn't be more thankful for the great life that hockey has provided for me and my family. But there were lessons from baseball that play into how I think as a hockey coach and one is the batting cage mentally.

Each spring, I always get excited when baseball returns and it starts with spring training. All the major outlets show clips from Florida and Arizona of Major League Baseball players returning to the field and getting prepared for the season and every year there's always one type of clip that remains consistent... major league baseball players hitting off a practice tee like it was their first time hitting a ball. When kids start playing baseball they all start in a league called T-ball. A T is a rubber stand that the ball sits on to make it easier for the kids to make contact and put the ball in play. Following T-ball, the kids progress to coach pitch, where the coach pitches the ball so that the batter can make contact before progressing to facing actual pitchers from the other team.

So here you are watching grown men making millions of dollars starting spring training by working in the batting cage and hitting off the tee. The reason that they are doing this is that to be successful as an athlete your foundation of solid mechanics must be in place. When a batter is hitting off a tee they can concentrate on the swing and all the mechanics of their body from the head to their shoulders to their elbows to their hips to their feet and how they all integrate to make solid contact. Not only do these multi-millionaires hit off the T in spring training but you will also always find a T in the batting cage at a MLB ballpark during the season.

Making sure that players are grounded in their fundamentals you can also look at a basketball player turned baseball player... turned basketball player... the great Michael Jordan. You may not know that Michael Jordan did the same thing every time he started a practice which was to practice making a simple chest pass. Making a chest pass is one of the first things that basketball players will learn when they start playing the game. So here you are with the greatest basketball player of all time making sure that his fundamentals are perfect before he starts working on anything else. Whether it is a baseball player, a basketball player, or any athlete if their fundamentals aren't right they will have problems down the road, and as a goalie coach it is important that you provide the training that is going to allow your goaltender to learn the fundamentals so that their mechanics and structure are in place for them to be able to perform on the ice.

Training fundamentals cannot be done in a short period of time. It takes a lot of training over a long period of time to train the fundamentals necessary for a goalie to have their foundation set. Picking a goalie company that focuses on mechanics and structure is key. The partnership between the goalie and the coach must be a positive one. The goalie coach and the environment should help foster passion for the position and the love of the game. You should not have to push your son or daughter to go to goalie training as they should look forward to the interaction they have with their coach and the joy of improving their skills and becoming better at their favorite sport.

Clinics and Camps

When it comes to goalie training there is a big difference between clinics and camps. How to view clinics is that they are a series of training events contained in a program that lasts over a prolonged period of time. For example, Stop It Goaltending provides clinics that we classify as programs once per week in eight-week sessions. There are six eight-week sessions over the course of the year. In our system, most goalies participate in three of the six sessions annually. Youth hockey organizations may provide a clinic on their ice with their coaches once per week during the season. The key to clinics are that they are done regularly over a long period of time and a clinic's success is retention while the key to a camp is the experience of participating in that camp.

Clinics: The reason why clinics are so important is that they provide consecutive and consistent training that result in the best retention. The only way a goalie learns is when the lessons are compounded and this is where the frequency comes in. Ideally, a goalie attends a goalie-specific lesson or clinic once per week throughout the season. This will allow a goalie to build from lesson to lesson and retain what they've learned. Some organizations prefer to offer their goalies clinics once every other week throughout the course of the season. Using this method they can stretch their dollar while still providing their goalies the instruction they need throughout the season. Naturally, training every other week compared to every week, their retention is not going to be the same and you can argue that it is less than half of what it is for goalies training every week. The reason I consider it less is because if a goaltender misses a lesson for any reason they will have gone a month in between sessions. If retention is all about compounding lessons and training muscle memory it makes it very tough on the instructor to be able to cement what they are teaching in the minds and bodies of the goalies.

Environment: For me too often a goalie coach is viewed by the parents as successful if the goalies progress well throughout the course of the clinics. As I mentioned earlier, in this day and age most goalie coaches are well-versed in the techniques and structure that have to be taught for a goalie to have success between the pipes. The issue comes down to how often and in what environment does the goalie coach get to train the goalies. If a goalie coach is provided to goalies once per week over a 24-week season chances are they are going to do a very good job. If a goalie coach is provided to goalies every other week over 24 weeks they may be able to do a good job but surely not as good as if they were provided to the goalies every week. If a goalie coach is provided goalies once every 3 weeks I have found that it is extremely difficult concerning retention and it's almost like you're starting from scratch each time you step on the ice for a lesson. If at all possible, either privately or through a youth hockey organization, the goalie's best option is to train once per week during the season.

The environment of training is also something that plays a big role in the growth of a goaltender and the passion that they will show for the position. The goalie coach to goalie ratio, therefore, becomes very important. The Stop It Goaltending ratio formula is two nets, one goalie director/coach, two shooters to four goalies. As stated earlier the reason why we find this formula works is that it is the perfect blend of personalized instruction and energy at a price point in which most families can afford. Therefore, for a goalie coach to be successful they must be in the right environment for the goalie to thrive. If a youth hockey organization hires a goalie coach and puts too many goalies on the ice it is not the goalie coach's responsibility at that point if the goalies are not progressing as quickly as hoped. Remember, a goalie coach can only be as productive as the environment in which they work. Therefore, the expectation of parents should coincide with what is being provided and if they deem it not sufficient for their son or daughter they should look outside the organization for private options.

Camps: Camps are traditionally held over the summer or during holiday breaks while the season is going on. As mentioned earlier, muscle memory can only be built through compounding training over a long period of time. Camps traditionally last for 4 to 5 days. The chance of a goalie to train their muscle memory in that short of a time period is difficult. The big reason to go to a camp or one-week summer program is to learn new progressive techniques and the experience of being around other motivated goalies and dedicated coaches. An older goalie may attend a summer camp or one-week program to work on something specific being offered such as structure. Specialty camps with a targeted curriculum can be a big asset to older goalies. The one-week summer camp environment also works very well for families with younger goalies that either can't or do not want to be going to the rink every week of the summer. The family may be away for the summer or they just want to make sure their children get a break from the game, play sports, and do other things.

What a goaltender doesn't get in weekly clinics is the time to spend half a day or the full day with other kids who love playing goalie and want to get better. There is a tremendous value to spending this time with other like-minded children and relationships that are born at summer camp often last a long time. Not only are the goalies on the ice together in a camp or one-week program they are also together doing off-ice, lecture, and video. It is often a junior or college goalie that is still playing that is responsible for the off-ice events. This allows the young goaltenders to interact with a mentor and be inspired by their passion for the position. Therefore, the summer camp isn't all about the coaching received on the ice or the coach who is doing the teaching but it's also the other staff members and primarily the interaction amongst the goalies. If you talk to either of my kids who are now 22 and 25 respectively they will tell you they still keep in touch with a bunch of the kids that they met through the Stop It summer programs.

So I'm sure you're wondering right now what I would recommend... sending your child to a goalie clinic or a goalie camp. If money, location and time are taken out of the equation I would recommend doing clinics for the retention and muscle memory and adding a summer camp or program to provide motivating experiences. One thing that I will tell you is that for an older goaltender the choice is rather simple. They need repetition and time to improve and therefore, a prolonged program is best suited for them. I believe at a young age a goalie that goes to a goalie camp or one-week summer program will enjoy the experience immensely and the passion derived from that experience will help fuel them to train and become a better goalie. Regardless, picking the ingredient has to stay consistent in either of the choices... and that is fun.

No matter if the goalies train in a clinic and or a camp environment if they are not having fun that is an issue. This by no means implies that they shouldn't be working hard and focus on their training but when they leave the rink, if they haven't been provided an opportunity to have some fun on the ice, that is going to be a problem. The issue is that without the fun element, going to training or summer camp will feel more like a chore than an enjoyable experience that they look forward to. One thing that has remained constant throughout the 20 plus years of Stop It Goaltending is that every session ends with game time. We have found that goalies will give you everything they have throughout the course of the session as long as you provide them with a game at the end which is free of coaching because of flat-out competition and fun. This results in the goalies feeling good about the training they received during their lesson and leaving with a smile on their faces because they got a chance to play at the end. I'm thoroughly convinced if we did not provide game time at the end of each session we would not be nearly as successful of a goalie development company that we are now.

Whether you are seeking a summer program for your son or daughter, it is important that you choose a program that will either benefit from a strong curriculum and retain the skills being taught or picking a camp or a one-week program that is going to provide a great experience. One thing that you may want to look at closely is who is providing the instruction and how much experience they have as well as what their reputation is. A lot of parents will choose an instructor or a program because of where the coaches have coached or whom they have coached in the past. I think it is very important to take a look at these things but as a goalie parent, it would be valuable to understand the difference between performance coaching and development coaching as they are two completely different skill sets.

Performance goalie coach and the development goalie coach: So what is the difference between a performance goalie coach and a development goalie coach? A performance goalie coach is typically a team goalie coach with a clear mission to help their goalies perform the best in the games. Traditionally, a goalie coach's responsibility is to the team or organization that they are working for. They are focused on getting goalies primed for games and that the goalie is giving the team a chance to win. Performance coaches work with their goalies in a team practice environment and therefore, their ability to impact mechanics is limited due to the fact they are working with the goalies in the season as opposed to the off-season. It is very difficult to train mechanics in a practice environment and there is traditionally not enough time before or after practice to properly train mechanics. As you know muscle memory can only be built over a prolonged period of time with compounding training. What a performance coach is very good at is analyzing the structure in which a goaltender plays and helping make adjustments to that structure to strategically play the game better. Performance coaches are also very good at the mental side of the game and help put the goalies in a state of mind that will allow them to be composed and confident while they play the game. A goalie parent cannot expect a performance coach to be able to dramatically impact the mechanics of a goalie during the course of the season and they must be fully aware of the fact that the performance coach's loyalty lies with the club and not with the goalie.

A development goalie coach is a goalie coach which is traditionally obtained by the parents of the goalie whose primary responsibility is the individual goalie that they are working with. A development goalie coach will traditionally be stronger at developing mechanics as this is their main focus and the environment in which they work. Development coaches are not traditionally at the games of the goalies and often do not have the opportunity to see them play. Traditionally a development goalie coach is working on mechanics and structure that would be applied in games. A development goalie coach is usually very good at breaking down each component of skills and understanding how to teach each of the skills using a teaching method that has yielded them the best results. It is helpful for parents of goalies to know that a development coach will have strengths and weaknesses that are entirely different from a performance coach and understand that the expectations of what their son or daughter are going to receive from each of these coaches are going to be different.

In an ideal world, a performance goalie coach has also been a development goalie coach as well so not only can they help prepare goalies for games but they can also spot any mechanical deficiencies that a goalie may have. Often a performance goalie coach is a former goalie that is coaching at a high level but may not have the experience of a development goalie coach that has worked with goalies of all age groups and needed to learn how to train a goalie that has never played goalie before and therefore not have all the nuances of teaching mechanics. You may find goalie parents choose a goalie coach because of where they played or where they coach although this coach may not necessarily be the best fit for what their goaltender needs at that particular time.

Whether they are a performance goalie coach or a development goalie coach, one attribute trumps all when it comes to selecting a goaltending coach for your son or daughter…and that is a coach that is passionate about the position and can pass that passion and enjoyment along to your goalie. Just because a goalie coach has coached or played at the highest levels does not mean that they have the skill set to pass this important ingredient to your goalie. Therefore, don't get swooped up by fancy titles but do your research by talking to other parents to find out if their young goalies were inspired, motivated and flat-out had fun learning this great position.

At Stop It Goaltending, we have a veteran coach by the name of John Carratu. If you mention John's name to a goalie he has trained, I will guarantee that just the sound of his name will bring a smile to the goalie. John was the goalie coach at Northeastern University and Merrimack College and did an exceptional job at each one of those schools. John coaches with as much effort and brings as much energy to an 8-year old that he does to a college star. Sometimes, I even have to wonder how many goalies come to see John each week because they want to become better goalies, or is it because they want to come and have fun while training! If you are fortunate enough to find someone like John for your son or daughter consider yourself to be lucky and enjoy the experience.

Learning Scales: You may at this point have provided your son or daughter with music lessons. Whether it be guitar or the piano or any other instrument, one of the things that each and every student has to learn are the scales. Scales are the foundation of being able to play well. If you are learning how to play the guitar it is essential how to hold the guitar and learn the notes before you learn the chords and songs. Learning goaltending is no different from learning the guitar. Without sound mechanics, eventually, a goalie's play is going to hit a plateau. Being a good goaltender is about being consistent. A coach has to trust the goaltender that they are going to give the team a chance to win every time they get on the ice. An inconsistent goaltender is going to make a coach question whether they should play and not allow the coach to concentrate on what he or she has to do. The only way a goalie can be consistent over a long period of time is to have the foundation of strong mechanics. Therefore, you can think of mechanics as learning your scales and we all know that mechanics can only be learned through compounding training over a longer time frame. A goaltender that strictly goes to camps for short periods of time is going to have a hard time cementing their foundation, aka... learning their scales. As a parent, this is something that we can look for and when finding the right mix of clinics and camps can determine what your goalie needs most and provide them with the training that will help them maximize their potential and enjoy the game.

Just Watch

I'm sure by now you may have heard about the 10,000-hour rule made famous in Malcolm Gladwell's book "Outliers." What Malcolm Gladwell explained is that it typically takes at least 10,000 hours of training in order to be elite at a particular skill such as an athlete or musician. An example he uses is one of the Beatles and how, as a band, they went to Germany and played in nightclubs with sets lasting up to 6 hours long. In golf, there's no one easier to look at than Tiger Woods and we all saw the videos of him as a toddler swinging a golf club. Earlier in this book we talked about the importance of games played and how many games Carey Price has played compared to other goalies his same age. For a goaltender to put in 10,000 hours, a component of it can be spent in front of the television watching NHL games.

There are only 64 goalies in the entire world that are capable of playing at the NHL levels and watching them play is a great opportunity for young goaltenders to see how it's done. Even better is the quality of viewing with

HD and flat-screen TV's or computers with exceptional quality. For young goaltenders watching the NHL'ers is an opportunity for them to learn how they play different situations and study mechanics. The one interesting thing that I've always said about summer training when kids from all over North America and Europe come to Stop It Goaltending is that we learn as much from the kids as they do from us. Being able to watch others do things that you don't see every day allows you to expand your horizons, learn new techniques and strategy and grow as a goalie.

The beauty of the NHL is that after each game on the NHL website they post a 3-minute recap of the game. What's perfect for the goalies is that the three-minute recap is 95% saves and goals against. It looks like it's made for a goaltender to enjoy, study and learn. Another opportunity that is fascinating for goalies is to watch the videos on the NHL.com website named "all of last night's goals". In roughly 5 to 7 minutes you can watch all the goals from the night before. If you don't have time to watch recap after recap this is a great use of time with a lot of benefits. The NHL also produces videos that are named "Top saves of the week" which is a bonanza of incredible saves by the world's best. At Stop It Goaltending we have a program called The Bridge for 13 to 15-year-old goaltenders who spend a full school year training and completing online school. Part of the program is, at noon every day, the goalies watch the prior night's games with Bridge coach and former NHL goaltender Andrew Raycroft. Not only do they just watch the clips but they also break down the goalies. About halfway through the year, it's as if the goalies don't even need Andrew Raycroft anymore as they are so in tune with how the goalies address the play. I would highly suggest to any goalie parent to encourage their kids to watch at least a few minutes each day on nhl.com.

[handwritten margin note: NHL.com]

Training Costs

I truly wish becoming a good goalie was as easy as signing up for a youth hockey organization and receiving the training necessary for a child to maximize their potential from that organization. In Europe, youth hockey clubs traditionally do a very good job providing qualified coaches consistently to their young goalies. Unfortunately, in North America, this is not always the case. If you are currently with an organization that commits to their goaltenders the training necessary for optimum development consider yourself very fortunate for the opportunity. If you are not currently in an organization that provides goalie-specific training you may want to consider seeking out training privately. Of course, private training is going to come at a cost. I cannot tell you what a competitive but fair rate for training is because each area is subject to its economics.

The cost of training is greatly influenced by the cost of ice time. At Stop It Goaltending we have tried to decrease the impact of the cost of ice by training in what we call development rinks. Development rinks are traditionally small ice surfaces and our rinks are approximately 35 ft. wide and 55 ft. long. We view our rinks as batting cages and because of the limited size, it helps control cost while providing goalies the curriculum we believe they need to succeed. These development rinks are therefore the equivalent of batting cages in baseball. Batting cages serve their purpose and are extremely valuable but obviously, you cannot train all aspects of playing baseball inside a batting cage and the same goes for our development rinks. If goalie training is conducted on full sheets and depending on what state, province, or country the rink is located it will greatly influence the cost of training.

The one thing that you have to consider when choosing training is the cost is what you will be able to provide from a frequency standpoint. As we have discussed in order to train muscle memory and retain that training it is essential to compound the lessons over a prolonged period of time. Therefore, when embarking on selecting a program it is important to consider how much you can provide your son or daughter because if the frequency isn't going to be there the retention is going to suffer. I know in my case both of my kids received very little one-on-one private training throughout their careers and opted for the small groups' lessons consistently.

The reason small group private training is so effective is the energy that is produced. At Stop It Goaltending we have four goalies and three staff members on the ice at one time. There are always two nets and the goalies that are not in the net are watching themselves on the iPads located right behind the shooters and the iPads are set on a time delay so the goalies can see themselves perform the drills without touching the iPads themselves. The energy level is a lot different than strictly a one-on-one private lesson. There is also a tremendous value for the goalies to watch each other so they are not only learning from the instructors but they are learning from the other goalies that they are on the ice with. Another great benefit of small group private lessons is game time. Game time is so much fun when four goalies are working their butts off trying to beat the shooters and having a ball doing it.

Small group lessons keep the cost down so that parents can afford twice the amount of lessons as privates. Some parents of goalies that participate in small group private lessons like to book the occasional one-on-one private lesson to address a particular skill, or situation, that their son or daughter needs to pay specific attention to. All in all, there is value to one-on-one private lessons and small group private lessons but from a cost standpoint, you may want to consider small group lessons and stretch your dollar a little farther.

Cutting Edge

As watching NHL videos is a tremendous way to absorb 10,000 hours necessary to become elite, virtual reality training is starting to become a viable way in which goaltenders can train. A company by the name of Sense Arena has developed an incredible platform in which goalies can see shot after shot and greatly improve without even stepping on the ice. I've been very fortunate to be part of the development team of Sense Arena and currently a goaltending advisor. My role has been to help develop drills to be goalie-specific that address areas where virtual reality can most add value. One area, in particular, that has striking applicability is screenshots. Something very hard to provide for goalies is practicing looking around the screen to find the puck. In a practice environment, players – for obvious reasons – don't want to be put in a situation where they could get hit by a shot and possibly injured. With Sense Arena, screening the player is virtual and therefore a goalie can take rep after rep of screened shots without anyone getting injured. Working on screened shots is just the tip of the iceberg of what virtual reality training can do for goalies.

1. Goalie Health.

While training on Sense Arena, goalies can pick either animated drills or actual video. Regardless of the drills, the one thing that remains constant is that the goalie does their training on their feet. This means a goalie can take a gazillion shots without ever going down which means there is no wear and tear on the hips and the knees which is great news for the goalie community. By staying on their feet, the goalies are working on their tracking skills and their reaction skills particularly with their glove and blocker. The focus on

143

the glove and the blocker allows the goalie to stay up over the puck and will help them better understand box control.

2.   Box Control.

To understand box control is simply adding a little geometry into playing goalie. So think about the size of a hockey net. Anywhere in the world, you will find that a hockey net is 4 ft. tall and 6 ft. wide. The Goalie stands in front of the goal so therefore the puck from its release point has to go by the goalie and into the net to score a goal. Now the area in front of the goalie that the puck has to pass is smaller than the net itself. We call this the box. So if a goaltender is at the top of their crease and the puck is being shot at from the blue line the shot cannot be higher than 3 ft. and 7 inches as it crosses the top of the crease or else it will end up going over the crossbar which is 4 feet high. As you can figure out, the goalie has an easier job protecting a net that is 3 ft. and 7 inches as opposed to protecting the net that is 4 feet high. Therefore, what the goalie is trying to do is stop the puck at the interception point of the box that is in front of them as opposed to the net that's behind them.

A good goaltender can make a living by focusing on stopping pucks from going through the box by keeping their shoulders square and filling the box with their equipment. How this applies to Sense Arena is that the platform offers goalies the option to display box control in the drills and that a goalie can see the small box in front of them where they have to make the save. Having this visual tool is a priceless feature that virtual reality has to offer that is not available in traditional training or practice situations.

3.   Reading the Release.

By training on the actual video option provided by virtual reality training at Sense Arena, a goalie can watch the actual release of a puck from a real shooter. Not only does the goalie see how the puck comes off the blade of the stick and predict where it's going to go, but they can also see the body language and movement that is involved in shooting a puck. Reading a shooter's body and how the puck comes off the blade over and over again will make it much easier for goalies to read the release of a shot when they face real competition. Once again the value of virtual reality training is that a goalie can see release after release after release without ever going down into a butterfly or an RVH and adding to the excessive internal rotations that goalies use every time they hit the ice.

4. Analysis.

Another great feature of Sense Arena is its ability to analyze how a goalie performs in a drill. Not only does it track how many shots a goalie saves within a drill it also allows a goalie to compete against other goalies in their age group but most importantly they can go back and see a 3D model of the shot that beat them and where it went in. So picture a goal that goes in high glove while training virtually. The goalie can go back and look at the puck that went high glove and then watch that 3D model of themselves and how the body moved to make the save. The goalie can then see whether they were too slow or too fast in trying to make the save and whether or not their glove position changed on the release of the shot or if the glove remained consistent in its positioning throughout the course of action.

5. Mental Game.

One feature of training virtually, is how it can impact the mental game of a goaltender. As I discussed earlier in the book, anxiety is an area that I struggled with as a goalie. When I turned pro and we had a morning skate the day of a game, it was a great relief for me because instead of worrying about the game the night before I knew that I had an additional skate the next

145

morning. This helped relieve some of the stress and anxiety. At the youth hockey level, goalies don't typically get the morning skate the day of a game. The beauty of Sense Arena is that a goalie cannot only make their morning skate; they can do it exactly when they want to do it and as many times or as long as they need. A goalie performing a few minutes of virtual reality training before they leave for the rink could produce a decrease in anxiety knowing that they can see some rubber before leaving for the game. I know that for me having a tool like this at my disposal would have greatly increased my enjoyment of the position.

It is so interesting to see how many pro goalies are using Sense Arena and virtual reality training to supplement their training. Some of the feedback that I have received from pro goalies is that they find that doing Sense Arena right before they go on the ice for practice allows them to see and track the puck better once they get on the ice. Therefore, what you are seeing now are goalies that get paid millions of dollars putting on their Oculus Quest and preparing to go on the ice. Development centers across the world are also training their goaltenders on Oculus Quest on synthetic ice sheets and even on real ice. At Stop It Goaltending headquarters located in Woburn, Massachusetts we have goalies going on the ice every Saturday afternoon to perform a virtual reality session. This works out great for our kids that may not have a game that day or don't want to get on the ice and get a workout in. I would encourage parents to take a few minutes to check out the Sense Arena website and find out more about the product.

Off-Ice Training

For any athlete to improve their performance on the ice, on the court, or in the field off-ice training is an essential component. When it comes to off-ice training there are many professionals in this space that you can consult and there are countless books and videos with professional advice on this subject. In this section, I will offer some suggestions based on my experience as a coach but not as an off-ice specialist. I would encourage that once an athlete hits high school that they select an athletic training facility and get a complete supervised program.

I think it's important to understand that a lot of what goaltenders are going to do off the ice is not specific to the position and is generic in nature. If a goaltender is getting the basic strength and conditioning program there is still a tremendous value in that. If a goalie can combine off-ice training that is geared specifically to their position then that's a home run. Learning about the different off-ice training opportunities in and around where a family lives may require some homework but it'll be worth the effort when you find the facility and training company that best suits your son or daughter. Typically, what you are looking for is an off-ice program that focuses on strength, agility and quickness, hand-eye conditioning, cognitive training, and flexibility...throw in some meditation and it's all covered.

1. Strength.

Several different strategies are used to develop strength in an athlete. There are some genuine concerns about some of the training that is considered generic that may not be in the best interest of a goalie based on the way that they play the game and the technique required to be a goalie. There seems to be an increased interest in pliability and a decreased use of the traditional Olympic training exercises. The easiest way to explain this is to think about the Olympic squat. These athletes put as much weight on a bar and perform a squat where they lower the weight into a squatting position and then raise the weight back to a standing position. Lifting this much weight puts a lot of stress on the body. A strength program that takes into consideration the needs of goalies may replace a full deep squat with the barbell with a one-legged squat where the athlete holds two dumbbells by their sides as opposed to a fully loaded bar up to around their shoulders. By performing a one-legged dumbbell squat a goalie is not only working on their strength and explosiveness but their balance as well with less strain on their hips and back. Using this example hopefully gives you an idea of what goalies are focusing on as opposed to simply seeing how much weight they can throw around during their workout.

2. Agility and Quickness.

An essential component to a goalie's off-ice training is agility and quickness. Balance is a big part of the agility quotient because without balance it makes it very difficult for an athlete to be agile. A goalie not only needs to add agility but they need to be quick as well. The strength training component of a workout should be geared to giving the goalie explosiveness in their game. Some goalies believe everything they do in the gym should be quick while others believe that controlled workouts that stress efficiency and economy of motion will translate well on the ice. In doing agility work it is important to first move in the correct patterns and then add speed once the patterns are done correctly. This is very similar to beginning strength training for a young athlete. New participants of off-ice programs typically start performing exercises with little or no weight so they can first learn how to do the exercises with proper form and once this is done they can add weight to increase the difficulty and improve the results of doing the exercise. There are agility drills galore on YouTube so a goalie has no shortage of drills.

3. Hand-Eye.

A great idea for a goalie is to add hand-eye coordination drills to their agility workout. Every goalie should learn how to juggle and once they get

148

this skill they can include it with their balance and agility exercises. It takes a little time to get the handle of juggling but once they figure it out it opens up a ton of possibilities for training. Tracking the puck is extremely important for a goalie so doing drills that require tracking on an object is perfect. When it comes to tracking you will probably hear a lot about convergence and divergence, the ability to track objects coming toward you and moving away from you. Anytime you are adding balls or objects to a workout you are also using these skills.

4. Conditioning.

Aerobic and anaerobic capacity is the third component of the off-ice program. One thing that you may want to take into consideration is that a goalie's conditioning needs are much different from players and often an athlete playing a different sport. Just think about how a hockey game goes and how busy a goalie gets. Often the goalie has a lot of activity in a short period of time and then a break while the puck goes out of their zone, to the far end, and back again. Therefore, a goaltender has a higher need for anaerobic training as opposed to aerobic training which means training at a high frequency for a short period of time with a longer break in between. No matter what, having some form of aerobic training mixed with the total plan is a good idea.

If you cannot find a program in your area or you are looking for something that you can do on your own that is goalie specific you have no reason to look any further than Maria Mountain. Maria can be found at Goalie Training Pro. Maria is the foremost authority on goalie training and her programs and videos have received rave reviews from goalies around the world. Not only does she have off-ice training programs for goalies to be performed in the off-season she also has in-season programs and specific drills and exercises to help goalies with things such as increasing the width of a butterfly. Maria, one of the best at what she does, is also a tremendous person who cares greatly for her clients and the product that she produces. It is great to have someone like Maria as part of the goalie fraternity and having the ability to have access to her programs online by virtually anyone in the goalie world.

5. Cognitive Training.

Twenty years ago, most athletes trained during the off-season either in their basement or at a local gym on their own. Now you'd be hard-pressed to find an elite athlete not training in a sport-specific training program or privately with a personal coach. What we are starting to see is that not only are goalies training on the ice and in the gym but they are also working on their processing speed through cognitive training. Cognitive training is simply being able to visually see a situation, process what needs to be done, and then perform an act appropriately, deliberately, and quickly.

When you think of an athlete that epitomizes someone that was not gifted with elite athletic ability but the skill to process at an incredible level, the name Tom Brady is the first on the list. Tom Brady is arguably the greatest quarterback of all time but was only selected 199th overall in the NFL draft. It is not hard to understand why he wasn't drafted higher when you see the film of him at the NFL combine. His body did not look like someone who trained a lot in the gym and he was the slowest quarterback of all the quarterbacks tested for that draft. What NFL teams failed to understand was how quickly he processed the play and his insatiable appetite to compete as well as his love of the game.

At Stop It Goaltending headquarters in Woburn, Mass we are fortunate to have a cognitive training company located in our building named the G-

Lab. The G-Lab stands for the Greatness Lab and it consists of eight stations utilizing the most state-of-the-art equipment available today. Before each station, athletes perform a SPIN protocol which consists of three parts... changing your posture, performing a breathing technique, and positive self-talk. Each station has its SPIN and performing SPIN along with cognitive training allows athletes to work on their mental game and confidence in conjunction with learning to process quicker. The combination of the two elements allows a goalie or any athlete the opportunity to improve their ability to perform under pressure.

6. Vision Training.

One beneficial aspect of cognitive training is the ability to improve spatial awareness and visual attributes such as convergence and divergence as well as peripheral vision. There are specific vision training facilities and programs that do a terrific job and are available in most metropolitan cities. There are also online programs such as Vizual Edge where goalies can train their vision from anywhere in the world. As a goalie parent, you may want to look around your area to see which programs are available to work on cognitive training skills. One annual test you may want to consider is an eye exam with an optometrist. Some schools offer annual eye exams but an optometrist may be able to spot underlying issues that a generic exam may not necessarily pick up. The great thing about most typical issues with vision is that they can be quickly solved through glasses or contacts or often within a series of 10 visits. Please note there can be substantial changes from year to year so an annual exam can prove to be quite helpful.

7. Flexibility.

For a goaltender, flexibility is not only important by giving goalies that extra reach to make a save but injury prevention is greatly improved with flexibility. If a goaltender is looking to improve their flexibility, yoga is what I have found as an ideal way to do this while adding core strength, balance, and spatial awareness. I remember reading an article in the Boston Globe about Tim Thomas when he discovered yoga. It quickly became popular with goalies. Not only does yoga have numerous physical benefits but it also does wonders for calming the central nervous system. The physical benefits include flexibility, balance, and core strength. Yoga also teaches practitioners how to breathe effectively and mindfulness will have relaxation and regeneration benefits.

At Stop It Goaltending we were fortunate to have a yoga instructor named Kim Johnson and her company "The Athletes Yoga" based here in New England. Not only does she help our goalies in the aforementioned areas but she also focuses on injury prevention which includes hip mobility. If you are a parent looking to add yoga as part of your son or daughter's training you should be able to find a studio nearby or one of the many programs online. From a practical standpoint, many of our elite goaltenders supplement their summer strength and conditioning program with yoga twice weekly over eight weeks.

8. Meditation.

Another off-ice training activity that has seen a recent boom is meditation. Mindfulness and staying in the present is such a big component of success between the pipes so meditation is a natural fit, particularly for experienced goalies. A simple search on YouTube will produce numerous options with respect to meditation and you could also find teachers in your area as well. At our Stop It Goaltending Complete Goaltending Summer program, we teach goaltenders the 24 forms of Tai Chi. Tai Chi is often referred to as walking meditation and I have found this form of training an ideal match for goalies. Tai Chi is a martial art that has participants slowly go from pose to pose, known as forms. The movement is fluid and you can even classify it as graceful. While one moves from pose to pose they are allowing thoughts to come and go and the ability to release the thought is truly a skill worth working on. Tai Chi can be practiced at anytime and anywhere independently or in a group.

The Combination: As you have read there is no shortage of training options that can be in addition to what your son or daughter may be doing on the ice and by no means would I suggest doing all of them. Finding the type of training that has the greatest positive impact on development will help goalies achieve their 10,000 hours to become elite at what they do. The best way to research these opportunities is to talk to other goalie parents and find out what they do. Getting connected with the family of a veteran goalie may help weed out some of the activities that do not help and identify the opportunities that may be at your fingertips. No matter what, you do not want to provide more than your child can handle, and always keep in mind that it is the enjoyment factor that will give them the drive to overcome any adversity that they may face along the way to becoming a goaltender.

Eat, Sleep, Fuel (Kelly Willing of UFIT)

When your child came into this world, you might have been more than a little obsessed with the amount of food consumed, weight gained, what was making its way into the diapers, all to ensure your child was hitting all their necessary developmental milestones.

Fast forward and your job hasn't changed much, except now you have a goalie and hopefully we are way past diapers. You should still be concerned about the quantity and the quality of food consumed, weight gained via muscle, bone growth and overall cognitive function. Solid nutrition plays a vital role in all of the above. Your child's brains and bodies will continue developing into their 20's and you want your student-athlete to be able to think and perform not only on the ice, but also in the classroom...and in life. Nutrition is the key to success.

The greatest goaltenders are just as disciplined off the ice as they are on the ice, and that discipline starts at a young age -- with you the parent. There's a lot of responsibility and pressure that comes with being a goalie, and the last thing you want to do is hinder your child's ability on and off the ice. Fuel and recovery are imperative for young athletes.

Food can be fun, but it also has an important job to do, it must sustain a young body through practices, training sessions and games. Hockey is a fast, rigorous, and physically demanding sport, with multidirectional movement, speed, agility, endurance, and strength - all while wearing bulky and heavy equipment. Aside from being physically strenuous, hockey also requires mental toughness. Hockey players burn between 400 and 1000 calories per hour. Now, it's not so surprising that your child is constantly hungry, is it? That being said, it is important to make sure you are giving them enough calories, in the right forms and at the right times to help their performance.

It's easy to say eat good food for good fuel, but it is a little more complicated than that. All foods can be broken down into three very important categories known as macronutrients. Carbohydrates, protein and fat. Let's take a look at our three macros, their simple functions and some examples of timing.

Carbohydrates

This is your fast-burning fuel primarily used for movement - our bodies convert carbohydrates to energy and we need energy to move. Carbohydrates are in just about everything from breads, pasta, fruits, vegetables, sports drinks, and virtually all packaged items. The List is seemingly endless. So, why not just eat a candy bar before the game and call it a day? Well, the proverbial 'junk food' is a lightning fast burn with no real nutrition. This can lead to an energy spike...and then a crash. With that crash can come lethargy, impaired cognitive ability, slow reaction times, maybe even nausea or a belly ache. So what are the carbohydrates you should be going for? Good sources of carbohydrates are breads, fruits, 100% real fruit juices and sports drinks. Just remember that carbohydrates pack approximately 4 calories per gram!

Protein

Protein is primarily for recovery and maintaining the muscles. Protein also helps to slow the burning process during your pregame fueling, but should be used minimally. Proteins are also vast and varied--everything from a hamburger, salmon, chicken, eggs, protein shakes and nuts are great sources of protein. For fueling purposes, the protein should be lean, clean and minimal for the best energy. Remember, food is fuel. We recommend nut butters on bread, eggs on toast, or a handful of nuts.. And if there's enough time before a workout or game, the bigger protein sources of chicken, beef and fish are advised. Protein packs approximately 4 calories per gram.

Fats

Fats are your slow-burning fuel source, and it is good to have combined in smaller quantities with your carbohydrates to help sustain energy for a longer period of time. Fats can be found pretty much everywhere as well. Examples include oils, nuts, nut butters, seeds, meats, eggs and some vegetables. It is important to get the right kinds of fat and to combine them with your carbohydrate sources. Good sources and use of fats for pre-workout/training/games would be nut butters on bread/apple, eggs and avocado on an English muffin or a small handful of nuts. Fats pack approximately 8 calories per gram! Yes, you read that right, which makes them "calorically dense."

OK, let's look at timing now. The following are suggestions for what to eat and when before getting on the ice depending on how full they want to feel. Note that these are general recommendations and vary greatly from person to person, so your goalie will have to experiment to find what works best for them. They may even find a combination of these snacks does the trick.

30 minutes before a session: Stick to the simple carbohydrates and aim for 15-30 grams or approximately 60-120 calories of breads, fruits and not much else. Stick to one or two slices of toast or an English muffin or a banana. Don't go overboard. Being too full will divert the body's blood supply to digestion and away from muscles and mind.

45 minutes before a session: This is a good time to add small amounts of fats and proteins to those carbs. Aim for 30-60 grams, but be careful with the fats (remember they are calorically dense). Try a smear of nut butter on that toast, or a small handful of nuts with your apple bumping your calorie total to approximately 150-300.

60 minutes before a session: Now you're getting far enough out to add some of that slow-burning food to the equation, maybe think of adding a hard-boiled egg. Try and aim for 300-400 calories.

Day of the game meal, 90+ minutes before the game: If your athlete is thinking about pregame at this time, you've got a hero on your hands. This far out, think about a piece of protein like chicken or fish to add to the mix. This can and should look more like a well-balanced meal than a snack. Aim for 400-600 calories.

The farther you get away from game time, the more you have to think about those quick-burn carbs as snacks (back to 30 min. and during). This is where your sports drinks and fruit slices come into play.

Notice we haven't talked much about vegetables. Of course veggies are the king, and queen and the whole royal court of solid nutrition. However, they are too fibrous for pre-workout eating. It takes our digestive system too much energy to break down that fiber and thus diverted much needed blood flow and energy away from where we want and need it. Save the veggies for well before or after your sessions.

Now let's talk quickly about maintenance and recovery. Your goaltender has just physically stressed his/her body, and those muscles are worn down, tired and sore. It is just as important to refuel their body immediately after their session with good fuel as it is beforehand - and this time it should be mostly protein! This is where protein shakes, smoothies and ready-made snacks show their value. This should happen within 30 minutes post session.

Recovery also takes rest and specifically sleep. During their advised 8-10 hours of sleep, muscles are repairing themselves and even growing. Former New York Rangers goalie Henrik Lundqvist required himself to achieve 9-10 hours of sleep each night and his diet consisted of 'carbo-loading.' "Sometimes it feels like the only thing you do is play hockey and eat," Lundqvist said.[1]

What goes into your goalie directly influences what comes out, just like when they were a baby. Good well-balanced and well-timed nutrition, rest and recovery goes in, resulting in a strong goalie coming out. Wayne Gretzky

---

[1] Bernard, Sarah. "Regime - New York Rangers Goaltender Henrik Lundqvist's Workout Plan -- New York Magazine - Nymag." New York Magazine, New York Magazine, 6 Apr. 2006, nymag.com/health/features/16629/.

claimed "The highest compliment that you can pay me is to say that I work hard every day, that I never dog it."[2] Great hockey players and goalies are not born from intrinsic skill, they must do their part and put the hard work in. They must never 'dog it.'

While the glory and excitement of being a goaltender is on the ice, it's what happens off the ice that forms the building blocks for being able to achieve that glory and excitement.

Until your goalie ships off to college, joins the NHL or starts a life of their own, their "eat, sleep and fuel" routine are still on you. Don't let them down.

---

[2] "Wayne Gretzky Quotes." BrainyQuote.com. BrainyMedia Inc, 2021. 1 July 2021. https://www.brainyquote.com/quotes/wayne_gretzky_166052

Goalie Parent Interview #5: Chris Knight

Spencer Knight is a 2001 born goaltender who was the 13th overall pick at the 2019 NHL draft and recently made his first NHL regular season and playoff appearance for the Florida Panthers. He played prep hockey for Avon Old Farms in Connecticut and for the Mid Fairfield Rangers before moving on to the US National Development Program where he led the US U18 team to the World Championship bronze and silver medal in back to back years. At Boston College, he was a first-team All-American and top 3 Mike Richter award finalist. At the World Junior Championship in 2020, Spencer excelled once again and posted a 2-0 gold medal shutout vs. team Canada.

When did your son decide to be a goalie?

Spencer first became a goalie at the age of five. Although he caught left-handed all they had for equipment were traditional sets with the glove on the right hand so that's how he learned to play. At one point he switched back to being a player but the new goalie struggled so the coaches convinced him to return to the net. It was a great situation in which he played out for the house team and goalie for the AAA program. He also loved playing out in lacrosse.

What did you feel about that decision?

I actually encouraged him to play goalie. The team needed a goalie and although I did not have much experience with the position, I knew that for some kids that some aspects may be hard to deal with but Spencer never got ahead of himself. He developed a tight relationship with Trevor Zegras and they played together all the way up until college.

What has been the best part of the journey so far?

The best part of the journey so far is the friendships and relationships that both Spencer and I have made through hockey. Because of all the travel, we have made a ton of friends and met people from all over the world. Playing youth hockey we traveled and spent a lot of time with other hockey people building lifelong relationships.

What has been the most challenging part of being a goalie parent?

The most stressful part of being a goalie parent for me is not being in control. It is similar to driving in a car going very fast. If you are the passenger it is stressful but if you are driving and you are in control then it's a whole different story. It's probably easier for our kids in net than us parents in the stands because they have that sense of control that we do not have.

What were the key aspects of his development that stand out to you?

For Spencer, he did not receive goalie lessons until he was a peewee. I think the fact that I was not a goalie expert helped because he had to figure things out on his own. He was really a self-taught goalie early on. The other thing that helped a lot was the sheer amount of games he played. The nice thing was that he loved to play and it gave him plenty of opportunities to learn the game and learn from his mistakes.

Do you get nervous watching games and if so how do you combat those nerves?

I think all goalie parents get nervous watching the game. I try to be calm and try not to get too high or low. I think if your goalies see you nervous up in the stands then they will be nervous too. For me, it's a little easier being at the game because there is more to do than waiting for it to come on television but I enjoy the TV games because of the multiple angles and replays.

What is one piece of advice you would give other goalie parents?

If I had one piece of advice to give to goalie parents it would be to enjoy the ride. It goes by quickly and if you add to the stress of the position it can weigh everyone down. It's easy to get caught up in the negativity and that can lead to burnout. Simply if you enjoy the ride the chances are they will enjoy the ride as well.

Step by Step

There's a famous expression when it comes to personal success and making it to the top... you're much better off taking the stairs than the elevator. By taking the stairs you have a chance to gain all the valuable experience that you will need when you get to the highest levels. When a goalie skips steps there is a risk of not gaining experience that they will need when they face adversity along the way. For goaltenders, this expression rings true and the next part of this book will walk parents through some of the situations that may occur specifically for each age group.

When my oldest son Joey was a peewee it was time for him to go to a new organization and play for a team that I didn't coach. In Massachusetts, we do tryouts in the spring so that the kids know where they will be playing the next season. Joey went on the tryout circuit which included trying out for a club program at the bantam level. We were both excited that he was able to make the teams that he tried out for including the team that played in an older age bracket. After much discussion, we decided that "playing up" would be a great opportunity. Ironically, that season ended up being the least enjoyable of all the seasons he played. Not only was he moving to a team that had already been together several years but he was also the youngest. Socially, he just wasn't ready yet to be with older kids and therefore impacted his passion and enjoyment for hockey. By no means am I saying that playing up isn't a good idea for some kids but it just wasn't the right choice for him at that time.

If we ever had the chance to talk one-on-one about goaltending I would be using the word "situational" a lot. Putting goalies in a situation to grow and develop not only as an athlete but as a person is essential for them. One

162

important job of a goalie parent is to try to put their son or daughter in a spot for them to succeed. Unfortunately, this often requires doing some legwork and making sure that the situation is the right fit for your child.

When I grew up, everyone simply played for their local town program and the best kids played for the area's AAA program. In New England, the privatization of hockey has led to competing club programs and therefore, players and families have the choice of club, also known as select, as opposed to their town. In some areas of North America, there are very few alternatives to play as it is the case in some European countries. When you do have a choice where to put your goalie, the situation that you put them in will be a major factor with respect to how they progress and the experiences that they have. Hopefully, some of the insight that I've gained from being a goalie parent myself and having been a coach and an owner of a private youth hockey organization, I can offer some advice that might help you make the right situational decisions for your goalie. I have this section divided into 5 groups.

- The Early Years (9 or younger) Learn to Play and Mite

- The Next Step (10-13 years of age) Squirt and Peewee

- The Middle Years (14-17 years of age) High School and Midget

- The Junior Years (18-20 years of age) Junior

- College or Pro (20 and older) College and Professional

The Early Years (9 or younger) Learn to Play and Mite

Every step along the way of a goalie's journey is important and the early years are no different. The first experience of playing goalie is the equivalent of how a first impression can be a lasting one. There are several questions you will ask yourself as a parent from learn-to-skate through mite and some hockey parents are new and do not yet have a lay of the land. If this is your situation, I would suggest speaking to a goalie family that has had experience in your area and can offer some practical advice.

How Do You Know?

How do you know if your son or daughter wants to be a goalie? Well, there's only one way to find out and that is to try. A lot of youth hockey organizations at the mite level use a rotating goalie system and each goalie is required to play goalie at some point during the season. All the kids get a chance and it allows each player to decide if a goalie is a position that they would like to pursue.

I will never forget my youngest son Alex's first game playing goalie. He played on a team where all the kids took turns being in net and one Saturday morning it was Alex's turn. Things didn't go well for his team that morning and Alex gave up 8 goals in the game. After each goal, I was thoroughly convinced that there was no way that he would want to ever put the pads on again. Following the game, I went into the locker room and he looked up at me with a big smile and said "Dad, can I be the full-time goalie". I had to laugh because this is the last thing I expected him to say but by being a goalie myself and knowing how much fun it is to stop a puck in a game environment... I guess I shouldn't have been so surprised. Therefore, the system of rotating goalies produced a newborn goalie!

A recent innovation that has proven to be extremely popular is what's called Quick Change Pads. These pads can slide right over a player's shin pads so, in a practice or skill session environment, players can switch quickly into goalie gear and do a drill as a goalie. The skill sessions are all a great opportunity for players to try being a goalie without having to play a game. The one thing about goalies is you do not want to force someone to have to be a goalie if they don't absolutely love it. Parents will quickly find out how much the kids love playing goalie by what they have to say following the practice or a game. Some parents will tell you they never want their kids to be a goalie because of all the pressure and adversity that might come from playing the position. We know that pressure is self-induced and life is all about perspective. If I wanted to do something, personally I would not be swayed because of what other people might think or say and I will do what I want to do. I feel the same way about our kids and their choices as we all want our kids to follow their path and do the things that make them happy and they're passionate about.

Full-Time Or Part-Time Goalie?

Once it is determined that your son or daughter is going to be a goalie here comes the subsequent question. Should they just play goalie or should they do both? There are a couple of ways that you can approach this. The number one skill a goaltender must have is skating and therefore playing out is a great way to improve as a skater. So if a six-year-old can play both positions he or she will be able to work on developing their skating skills, not only as a goalie but as a player as well. But what about if they only want to play goalie because they are so passionate about it and they are not interested in being a player? In this case, I have no issue with a goalie playing the position they love on a regular basis because this is how they have fun and enjoy the game.

Outside rotating players several scenarios have had success in developing goalies. The most prevalent is that there is only one goalie or there are two goalies on a team and they split each game down the middle. In this situation one goalie starts and the other comes in at the halfway mark and then the next game the goalie that played second now starts the preceding game. Another scenario is that there are two goalies on a team and when one of the goalies is in net the other goalie plays as either a defenseman or a forward. Especially in the early years, where wins and losses are not as important, this is a creative way to get the best of both worlds. Another scenario is for a goaltender to play on two teams, one team being the goaltender and the other being a player. This may not be financially an option or possible time-wise but that may be the best option. The one scenario that I have a lot of trouble with during the early years is having one goalie in net playing the full game and another goalie backing up the full game. I don't see the value of any young kid going to a sporting event and not playing but that's just my opinion.

Where To Play?

A lot of goalie parents face a difficult decision with respect to where their goalie should play. In the early years, most kids start off at their local program but decision time may come quickly depending on where you live. Of course, there are lots of different factors and each region has its own issues. There is a lot to consider when choosing a team during the early years such as location, the social aspect, the level of play, and so on. From my experience, the most important part of the early years is that the goalie is having fun and enjoying the environment that they are placed in. I don't believe that a goalie has to be put at the highest level of competition to improve at this age. What they have to do is foster the love of the game and enjoyment and respect for the position of goalie. Having them play goalie

166

with their friends and or classmates is a way for them to interact socially and enjoy what they are doing. A goalie that is put at a young age in an ultra-competitive environment may or may not have a positive experience. Of course, this is once again a very individual decision and you have to know your child and where they will be most successful.

I strongly believe that self-confidence is the key characteristic for success and if an athlete is over their head it will severely detract from the enjoyment of the sport and impact their long-term enjoyment and participation. Playing elite hockey or not between 6 and 9 is not going to determine a college scholarship. Of course, playing with better players will generally bring out the best in an athlete but we say "Play Hockey" for a reason. Playing is fun! To make it to the highest level of the sport the athlete is going to have to love their sport. As competition and pressure increase, the harder it will be. It is imperative that young goalies and players flat out have fun playing the game of hockey. It is the love of the game and positive memories and experiences that are going to pull them through the hard times.

As we discussed early on in the book, one important element of development for goaltenders is experience and the way to get experience is to play games and see a lot of shots. Playing for a team that wins every game with the goalie not getting many shots is not an ideal scenario. An argument for playing on a powerhouse team with excellent players is that the goalie increases the number of quality shots they face in practice even though they don't see them in a game. I look at this situation similar to teeing off in golf. If you're a golfer you know that teeing off on the first tee is much different from teeing off on the next 17. Typically, the first tee is around the clubhouse and often some people are watching as opposed to the next tee where it's just the players you are golfing with. Stopping pucks in a game is equivalent to hitting off the first tee in golf. Taking shots in practice is the equivalent of holes 2 through 18.

An ideal situation for goalies would be to be able to play on a competitive team where they would see a good amount of shots and still have a chance to win but not be dominant. If your son or daughter ends up on a team that is very weak and has very little success here is an approach you can use to keep their spirits up. You can break the game down into three mini-games. Therefore, you and your goalie can take a look at each individual period within a game and see how they did that period. Therefore, although they won't technically win many actual games they have the opportunity to win the mini-games and even get shutouts. Playing mini-games also gives a goalie a fresh mindset each time a period starts because they have a new chance at a new game

Regardless of a decision on where to play, part of being a goalie parent is to make sure that it is fun for our goalies. We want so much for them to do well and carry the team but this may not always be the case. Make sure that results are not the emphasis but development is the key. A growth mindset as opposed to a fixed mindset will more or less determine if it will be a positive experience. A growth mindset means that every experience, good or bad, will lead to becoming better at playing goalie. A fixed mindset could end up in "I am not good enough". Parents have a huge influence on the mindset of their children. Babies exhibit a growth mindset or a fixed mindset as early as one to three years of age. Make sure your goalie understands every experience is an opportunity to get better.

Tournament Teams

As goalies get older you'll find that the number of off-season tournament options increases rapidly. There are typically not as many tournaments for younger teams. The advantages of tournaments are that it gives goalies extra games played and therefore they become more experienced, it also may allow a goaltender to play at a potentially higher level and therefore stiffer competition. I did not have either of my boys play any of the off-season mite tournaments as that time was reserved for soccer and T-ball. As your son or daughter starts to get a little bit older, adding off-season tournaments is a way to not only have them improve and increase visibility but it is also a great time to bond with friends.

Tryouts

If you were going to have your son or daughter play for a club or select team or a team outside their area they will probably have to attend tryouts. I'm a big believer in the value of trying out because it's a great way to prepare the kids for what they are going to face later on in their career and in life. A lot of kids, if they're nervous when it comes to trying out and at a young age, take it hard if they don't make the team that they are trying out for. This is a great opportunity to polish up your parenting skills and talk them through it. The most important thing about a tryout is the word try. What they should be proud of, whether they make the team or not, is that they put themselves in the position of trying. If you remember the definition of confidence as being "the ability to act" then they in essence have grown in confidence regardless of if they make the team or not.

One thing to keep in mind when it comes to tryouts is that goaltending is not golf. If you go to a golf tryout it is pretty simple... the player that shoots the lowest score wins. Goaltending, unfortunately, is not that clear. In a tryout situation, a goalie that lets in more goals than another may still be selected for the team because a coach feels that they have more potential than another goaltender. This becomes difficult for goalies and their parents to understand.

Whether the coach selects a goalie because of projection or any number of other reasons over another goaltender it is important to understand that the decision is simply based on an opinion. It's not a fact and therefore just because a goalie does make it doesn't mean that they weren't better than the goalie that didn't make the team. It's just the opinion of the person that decided on who was going to be the goalies. Just think about a presidential election where you have half the country believe that one candidate is better than the other. You don't know who the right one is, but it is their opinion.

If a goalie doesn't make a team, parents and goalies often look for answers. Were the other goalies quicker, better trained, had better rebound control, or were more athletic or competitive? In my experience, there is not a lot to be gained by questioning the decision of the coaches. As I mentioned, it simply comes down to one person's opinion and therefore, in all reality you are basing your son or daughter's qualities on what that one person thinks. What a goalie should take away from not making the team is the desire to improve their game and make the next one.

Making The Team

When a goaltender makes the team, especially for the first time there's a lot of excitement about the process. They should be very proud of themselves but especially proud of having the courage to go through the tryout process. After tryouts and your goalie has been selected for a team and before committing to that team parents may want to think about whether you want to contact the coach with respect to the protocol in which the goalies are going to be handled during the season. Each organization and team within an organization may have separate protocols for playing time and therefore development of their goaltenders.

If your son or daughter is going to be the only goaltender it is important to understand what the expectations are regarding practices and games. If there's only one goaltender on a team and that goalie is unavailable for practice it limits what the coach can do with the rest of the players and what happens if the only goalie on the team is going to have to miss a game because of a family commitment, academic conflict or health issue. Before committing to the team it is important to have a conversation with the coach to be clear about the expectations of your son and daughter and the protocol regarding potential missed events.

If your son or daughter is going to be one of two goalies on a team it may be a good idea to speak with the coach about ice time before committing to a program and how the allocation of ice-time will be divided between the goaltenders. Will it be an equal distribution where goalies play half the game or will it be a play-to-win team scenario or a hybrid of the two. Ice time on a play-to-win team is allocated by the coach based on whom they think has the best chance to win and therefore when accepting a spot on a play-to-win team a goalie and goalie parent must understand that they may receive limited ice time.

Most teams play tournaments during the year and they are a great chance for the players and the parents to bond and enjoy a mini-season before, during, or after the regular season. Much like the importance of a parent to understand how ice time is going to be distributed during the regular season it is also a topic that should be discussed. Even teams that rotate their goaltenders in a set way during the season may vary when it comes to tournaments. Therefore, the coach may rotate the goalies in the round-robin portion of the tournament but when it gets to the playoffs they are going to play the stronger goalie.

In addition to getting a clear understanding of ice time allocation and absences, it may be a good idea to inquire about what exactly the organization and team are providing for in-season training for their goalies. Some organizations provide a lot of training while others provide none at all. So going into the season you may need to supplement your goalies' training but before you do that you may want to ask what is being provided, by whom, and at what frequency.

Whatever the protocol is going to be for the goalies the time to have the conversation is before joining the team. Having a conversation about ice time after the season has started will put the goalie and the parents as well as a coach in an awkward situation. The last thing you want to do is have this conversation in the parking lot of a rink after your son or daughter did not play in a game. It is much better to have this conversation before agreeing to join the team than once the competition begins. One approach which has worked very well for some of the parents and I have advised after they have the conversation with the coach and clearly understand the expectations, is to take a few minutes to send an email to the coach going over their understanding of how the season is going to run with respect to the goaltenders and what they understand the expectations are. By no means is this a contract but at least if there is a situation that arises during the season you can refer to the email as a point of reference which may help clear up any misunderstandings.

Next Year

At least in New England one of the amazing phenomena in hockey is the next year mentality. What this means is that the minute January 1st comes around the parents and players start talking about where they are going to play for the next season. This phenomenon is reserved for areas where there are options for the players and the families. During this time, it is important to remember that, despite the talk about which player is going to which team, learning to play in the present and be where your feet are, are essential qualities of a goaltender. A goaltender moving from team to team is not as easy as a player. In my experience, for a goalie that jumps from team to team trying to look for a better situation is not necessarily the best approach. The goalie does not need to be on an elite team to improve, they just need to see competitive shots in live games.

Training

Parents have a few different strategies of how much, if any, the training they should provide during the early years. You can either wait until you are sure your son or daughter is committed to being a goalie before including position-specific training or get right after it. A staple diet of training for a goaltender typically consists of one goalie-specific lesson once per week or once every other week during the season and summer. A third option which may seem a little counterintuitive at first would be to provide a lot of training at a very early age.

In 2015, USA hockey did a study to determine when the optimal window of trainability is for hockey players. What came out of it primarily is that the peak window is between the age of 13 and 15. My company even designed the Bridge Program around this study where we provide a comprehensive 38 week on and off-ice training program for 8th and 9th graders. But what gets overlooked in that study was there were two peaks and the second one was at... you guessed it. Six years of age.

When my older son Joey was six he wanted to be a goalie and a player and that was fine with me but I did say that if he wanted to play goalie I would teach him the fundamentals before even starting with his team. That decision was made a long time before the USA study and my decision to train him right away was based on no previous theory or philosophy. I can tell you now that it is likely the best thing that I ever did for him and here's why.

With no bad habits and muscle memory to change I was starting with a blank slate. At six years old a goalie is learning how to stand and move using proper mechanics. Any language teacher will tell you that the younger the student the easier it is for them to learn. Why should it be different for athletes? The fact that he did his training early solidified his muscle memory actually meant that he could do less training and more playing as the years progressed.

When a parent asks me when to start goalie training I say as soon as possible. Of course, it sounds disingenuous because I am in the business of training goaltenders but I do know that getting the fundamentals down early for a goalie can deliver long-term results. Of course, this may be contrary to everything you will hear but I can tell you that it was very beneficial for Joey and a number of other goalies that have taken this approach.

Whichever way you go when deciding what to provide your son or daughter it is important to remember the 13 to 15-year-old optimal window of a trainability period. Something that will help you identify how much you should be doing with your goalie is their enthusiasm level. If you are dragging them to training then you will know to back off but if they keep asking for more than it gives you the green light to put them in a situation to get better.

Equipment

You probably heard by now that the cost of playing goalie is a factor in playing the position. The great thing about most youth hockey organizations is that they typically provide equipment for goaltenders at the youngest ages. Each organization usually has a stash of goalie equipment that they give out at the beginning of the season to each team and it is the team and not the parent that is responsible for providing the equipment. The good side of this is that the equipment is free but in certain situations, you may find that it is outdated or doesn't fit well.

When it comes to choosing equipment at any level, protection is the most important ingredient. If a goaltender isn't protected, the puck will find its way to hit exposed parts of the body and therefore, will lessen the enjoyment of playing. Once a goalie gets hit a few times and feels pucks hurting them, they will naturally start to be more timid. You can't blame the goalie that isn't protected and is getting hurt by shots to be more concerned about protecting themselves than actually making the save. As a goalie parent, you want to make sure the equipment that your son or daughter uses is safe enough for them to go out and enjoy themselves or you'll quickly find them exit the crease.

If the equipment being supplied is not at the level that protects your goalie you can also take it upon yourself to go out and buy equipment. What a lot of people don't understand is that equipment at the youngest levels is very affordable. I can tell you that I am impressed with the equipment manufacturers as the quality and price point starter goalie sets are very low. It may be worth a trip to the hockey store to see what they have and I think you'd be pleasantly surprised at the sticker price. If you're buying goalie-specific equipment for your goalie you are going to need pads, a blocker and a glove, a chest pad, and a helmet/mask. The rest of the equipment such as skates, pants, and the helmet can be the same as a player although there are also goalie-specific skates.

Often for goalies just starting, a big question is whether to buy goalie skates or player skates. If your goalie is 100% into being a goalie then goalie skates make a lot of sense but if they are going to go back and forth you may want to stick with player skates to get started. The difference between player skates and goalie skates, along with protection, is the rocker that is put on the blade itself. As a goalie commits to be a full-time goalie, a pair of goalie skates is going to be necessary.

One of the coolest things about playing goalie is the mask. Mask manufacturers much like the equipment manufacturers themselves are doing a great job of being able to provide goalie masks that have cool designs at an affordable price. If your goalie is also playing out you may want to consider the standard helmet and cage combination that they can use as a player or a goalie. Regardless of which option you choose, I would encourage you to have your son or daughter use a throat protector, often referred to as a dangler, which is the plastic piece that hangs off the helmet or mask to protect the neck area, as well as a neck guard which protects against lacerations.

Ironically, one of the biggest decisions that you're going to have to make is the paddle height of a goalie stick. This is why it's important when purchasing a stick you bring your goalie's gear with you to the hockey shop so that they can put on those skates and equipment and a salesperson can help determine the height of the paddle of your goalie stick. The paddle is important because it will impact how a goalie will stand in their stance and a paddle that is too high or too low can have a dramatic effect on how they perform. On another note when it comes to choosing a stick and paddle height is that the paddle height is not consistent from manufacturer to manufacturer. Therefore a 24-inch paddle in a Bauer stick may not be the same as a 24-inch paddle Warrior brand or CCM stick. Just make a note when you are going to buy goalie equipment that you packed a bag beforehand and bring their equipment whether it is purchasing a stick or other pieces of equipment, they must work together, and therefore it is important to try on the new pieces and see how they function with the old ones.

The Break

Regardless of how much or how little training they did, something that I always insisted with my kids was to give them a minimum 8-week break in between the season and summer goalie camps. There are a couple of reasons why I did this and recommend that all goalies should take the same break as well unless they can't train in the summer. My feeling is that if a goalie doesn't get away from the rink it will impact their passion for the position and excitement to go play. A lengthy break between the completion of the season and when they're going to jump on the ice with their buddies at goalie camp will keep them hungry to continue to grow and enjoy the positions for sport.

Taking time away from the ice in the spring allows the kids to play other sports and learn how to move their bodies in different ways. Figuring out strategies in those sports will help a goaltender to be better at reading the play and simply... figuring out the game. With the wear and tear on the body of a goaltender, especially the hips, and the compounding of internal rotations performing the butterfly, an 8-week break it's just what the doctor ordered.

Break for me means no hockey whatsoever. What that means is that if you get a phone call after week three and a coach needs a goalie for a tournament and they are desperate… you simply have to tell them your son or daughter is not available. During break time, it is essential to stay away from the rink so that you don't get the sights, sounds, and smells of a hockey rink for at least two months. If your family is one to go on summer vacation and therefore cannot provide summer goalie camp then you may want to consider training in the spring and taking the whole summer off from hockey.

Goalie Parent Interview #6: Jim Burt

Katie Burt is a 1997 born goalie and the all-time winningest female goaltender in NCAA college hockey history. She was the first overall draft pick of the NWHL in 2017 and is currently a member of the Boston Pride. A native of Lynn, Massachusetts, Katie played prep school hockey for Buckingham, Browne, and Nichols and for the East Coast Wizards club program. At Boston College, Katie recorded an undefeated season in 2015 and won the Hockey East Championships in both her freshman and sophomore seasons. Internationally she played for the United States Women's National U18 hockey team in both 2014 and 2015, winning a silver and gold medal respectively. On top of playing hockey professionally and goalie coaching, Katie is a ball girl for the Boston Red Sox.

When did your daughter decide to be a goalie?

Katie began playing hockey because the kids in the neighborhood playing street hockey asked her to play goalie. She loved it and that was the start of it all! She then played Mite B her first year and the following season moved up to the Mite A team. At the squirt level, she began to play on two different teams where she would play for a boys' team as a goalie and then on a girl's team she would play both goalie and out. Whether she was playing with the boys or the girls it was fine with me, she just loved it and had so much fun.

What did you feel about that decision?

Quite honestly, I had no reservations whatsoever about her playing goalie. She was really into it and I thoroughly enjoyed it. Regardless of the early mornings, the late nights, and the travel, those were actually the best times and I would go back and do it all over again in a heartbeat. Katie was just so competitive even at an early age I enjoyed watching her play and fortunately for me and her mother, she seemed to be on the winning end much more than she was on the losing end!

What has been the best part of the journey so far?

The best part of the journey for me has been the incredible moments that we shared together whether it was in high school, college, or playing for the national team. All those great battles internationally against Canada were just incredible hockey and so much fun to be a part of. Just being able to experience some of those dramatic events I'll never forget.

What has been the most challenging part of being a goalie parent?

I say the most challenging aspect of being a goalie parent it's just feeling helpless when they are out on the ice. Sometimes you wish you could just hop on the ice and give them a hug or some words of encouragement. That of course we save for the ride home or some quiet time at the house but when it's happening live you just want to be there to support them.

What were the key aspects of her development that stand out to you?

We were fortunate when Katie was about 12 years old to have the ability to send her to goalie-specific training. I really didn't know about the options up to that point and if I did I would have had her start earlier. Katie lacked a little in the skating department. I think if she would have had the chance to learn how to skate better as a goalie at an earlier age she could have even had more success. Finding specific training played a big role in her success and she still continues to train religiously to this day.

Do you get nervous watching games and if so how do you combat those nerves?

I guess I may not be the typical goalie parent because I've never really been nervous watching Katie play. If you ask my wife you may get a completely different story and maybe it's because Katie had so much success and was lucky to win a lot of games but I never look at it as something that should be stressful and it's just not in my nature. As some parents like to stand on their own and not hear the discussions and the comments made by other parents during the game, once again this may not be typical, but for me it was part of the experience that I really appreciated. I enjoyed being in the thick of things and the relationships that I had with the other parents. I always had a lot of belief in Katie and was never worried that she wasn't going to try her hardest and therefore just went to the games and enjoyed myself.

What is one piece of advice would you give other goalie parents?

Although it may sound easy, the one piece of advice I give goalie parents is to enjoy the journey and the process. At the end of the day, the kids are just playing a game and the game is supposed to be fun. This isn't real life. Therefore, I never got myself worked up over wins and losses and performances. If I could pass along one thing to the other goalie parents it would be to keep the game in perspective.

The Next Step (10-13 years of age) Squirt and Peewee

As a parent what we try to do is provide our kids with the opportunity to try multiple things including multiple sports. After they have been exposed to the different options of what they may want to play at an early age they will start to gravitate with what they enjoy the most. Ironically what they tend to enjoy the most are the things that they do well and therefore if your son or daughter is having success between the pipes there's a good chance that they want to continue to the next step. The next step in the life of a goalie is the 10 to 13 years age group which in my area is referred to as squirt and peewee.

How Do You Know?

After the early years, most teams start to gravitate away from the rotating goalie concept and have either one or two goalies per team. You may be faced with the question of whether your son or daughter should remain a goaltender only or choose to be a player. This may seem like an easy question for some kids and hopefully, that's the case but it could also be a difficult decision and one that is hard to turn back from a couple of years down the road.

This decision was one that I faced with my son Joey a little bit later because he was playing on two teams, one as a player and one as a goalie. I remember sitting in his room and having this very conversation. By no means did I want to influence his decision either way as I know it is the passion that is going to help them down the road and I wanted to make sure that it was his decision and him following his passion. For Joey it was really interesting how he came to the decision... he said, "Dad, I love playing both player and goalie but I think I am a much better goalie and if I want to make it to Boston College and the Boston Bruins I have a better chance as a goalie". Well, he never made it to Boston College but he did sweep them his junior year as a goalie at ASU and although not playing for the Bruins he hopes to play against them as a member of the Seattle Kraken.

So Joey based his decision on a dream and aspiration which is one way to look at it. I can't say he was wrong about his assessment of being a better goalie than a player but I wanted to make sure that it came from him. In most cases, it will come down to what position they enjoy the most. As a parent, they'll be more challenges if they choose to go down the road as a goalie but if you're like most parents we will do anything we can to support our kids and help them chase their dreams. When having this discussion and making the decision the issue is if you choose to become a goaltender during this age group or a player and then two years down the road change your mind, it will be tough to make up those two years of development. If somehow a goalie can play at a good level as a goaltender and also play out this is also an option worth exploring.

Full-Time Or Part-Time Goalie?

As I mentioned earlier, there are typically no more rotating goalies during the next step and teams mostly have one or two goalies that are set for the season. At the highest level of this age group, teams may be adapting to the play to win mentality which is to earn your ice time. At the squirt and peewee age group, a goalie has to start thinking about being a regular. That being said, what I mean by a regular is that they are playing either in every game or every other game if they're playing out. As I mentioned before, I prefer when a goalie goes to a game they play at least half of that game. At this age group, the coach may feel it is better for the goalie to play full games and rotate games as opposed to change halfway through the game. Although this is not my suggestion, parents should know before the season how ice time will be distributed and therefore understand the rules before playing the game.

Where To Play?

In the early years, getting on the ice, having fun, meeting new friends, and learning a new sport are the goals. While moving to the next step, choosing a team starts to increase in importance to goalies and parents that are motivated to put themselves in the best situation to maximize their potential. A great spot for a goalie is to play for a competitive team where they are going to see plenty of ice time and shots. In my opinion, it is not essential to play at the highest level but as a goalie to be the best they can be, you want to put your goalie at a level that they are being challenged. In addition to choosing a regular-season team, there are also opportunities to play for tournament teams in the off-season.

When my oldest son Joey was between the age of 10 and 12 he never played at the highest level in his age bracket. Although not with the top elite players in his age he did play on a competitive team where he faced a lot of shots and received plenty of ice time. By no means do I suggest not playing at the highest level if your son or daughter is capable of it but my point is that just because they are not playing at an elite level during this age group does it mean they do not have the potential to have a long and successful goalie career. Once again for every goalie, their path is going to be different and as a parent, we are just trying to find the best situation for our kids given their skill set and passion.

Tournament Teams

At this age group, I typically chose anywhere from 1 to 3 tournaments in the summer for my kids to play in. Combining summer tournaments and training allows the kids to not only develop new skills but implement what they are learning at summer camp in a game environment. Off-season tournaments for 10 to 13-year-olds are a great way for goaltenders to get additional games, potentially face stiffer competition, and have a lot of fun. There are local tournaments where the level may be similar or a little stronger than what your son or daughter may see during the regular season. In considering time & expense local season tournaments are a quick and easy way to get on the ice in the spring or summer without breaking the bank.

There is a subculture in hockey which is the elite tournament circuit which is born at this age level. Even as someone that was in the youth hockey business at the time, being exposed and understanding how this circuit works took some time. There are a number of high-level tournaments reserved for very competitive teams of strong players who travel from hockey hotbed to hockey hotbed and play weekend tournaments. If you live in one of the areas that put together these elite teams and you are a very strong goaltender you may be approached to play on one of these teams. If you are looking at games for your son or daughter and have them challenged against the best of the best, these tournaments are a great opportunity.

Regardless of whether you're playing at a local tournament or are catching on in the elite tournament circuit, it is important to take the 8-week recommended break for goalies. What I did with my kids is limit the off-season tournaments to three with one of those tournaments being at a very high level and the others local. I wanted to make sure both Joey and Alex had time away from the rink to recharge their batteries, play other sports and participate in other activities...basically, be a kid. A lot of the decisions of whether to play off-season tournaments and what level to play are dependent on the level and the activity involved on a goalie's team. They may play on a team that plays a lot of games during the regular season and therefore, there is no need to play in the summertime or they may play on a team that does not play as much or does not play at a very high level and therefore experience and competing against the better competition can be obtained during these tournaments.

Tryouts

Tryouts for squirt and peewee teams start to get a little bit more intense than in the early years. Typically, the kids and the parents know the competition that they are up against and the dynamics start to change quite dramatically. While in the early years' accolades go to the goalies for taking the action for trying out, goalies in this next phase of development, should be encouraged not only to take action of trying out but to understand the importance of having a competitive spirit. Sport has always been considered a microcosm of life and as parents, we look for opportunities to teach and have our kids grow from the experiences they have while on the ice, court, or field. When it comes to tryouts the kids have to understand that they are competing and not just out with their buddies going to practice. Praising your son or daughter for not only getting on the ice but understanding that they are competing is important.

One way to look at tryouts that I found to be effective is that the goalie they are competing against is themselves as opposed to the other goalies on the ice. Much like the analogy of a goalie being like a golfer and competing against the course as opposed to the person that they are golfing with, a goalie should be concerned with their performance as opposed to anyone else's. Why they make the team or not is simply the opinion of one person and getting caught up and how the other goalies are performing during the tryout will only pull your goalie's mind away from concentrating on their game and simply stopping pucks. There are a lot of distractions when it comes to tryouts such as new kids, new format, sign-in process, and getting a penny, the chatter in the locker room...etc. and they can all impact the focus of the goalie. As long as your son or daughter goes out on the ice and competes to the best of their ability free of distraction then they have won. If they are on the ice trying to play for the evaluators and questioning how they look or if they are doing well it can be an uphill climb. A great saying to use during the tryout is "Never get beat twice" as this will allow them to give up a goal and bounce right back and make the next stop.

As a parent during tryouts, I would reiterate the same advice as earlier in this book about finding a spot to watch, staying in that spot, and supporting your child. As opposed to a typical game situation it is not the norm for parents to cheer for their kids while they are on the ice trying out for a team.

A parent can simply relax and watch the tryout and be proud of their goalies' effort and confidence to act. Parents should refrain from interacting with the coaches or evaluators while at the tryout. They are focused on trying to evaluate all the players and orchestrate the actual tryout itself.

One thing to keep in mind in the tryout process is that you will be watching every save that your son or daughter makes and every goal they may or may not give up. We like to think that the evaluators see the same thing but you may want to keep in mind that the evaluators are also trying to see all the other players and therefore when your son or daughter makes a great save no one other than you may be watching. If the tryout process is successful or not is up to how you would like to perceive it. As in the last chapter, the true winner of the tryout is the goalie that puts themselves on the line, demonstrates the ability to act and competes to the best of their ability and the result will be that their confidence and determination will grow.

Next Year

When you are in the 10 to 13-year range things get a little bit more interesting when it comes to selecting a team and deciding where to play. At this point, parents are more open to driving further distances if it means the right situation as once again it's the situation that trumps all and putting your son and daughter with a team that they will be able to grow and continue to develop. Like I said before, for me playing on the best team is not necessarily the best thing for a goaltender. Finding that team which is competitive and where you can make a difference could be a great development experience.

What is also apparent is that coaches are starting to figure out at this point who the stronger players are and trying to recruit them. When parents ask me about moving teams, the first thing I do is ask them what their current situation is. The grass isn't always greener on the other side as the saying goes and I have seen too many parents leave a situation where their child is progressing and enjoying the position and sport only to find themselves with the team that they are not happy with. Before looking elsewhere you may want to get a good understanding from the coach of what is expected for the next season and see if that matches up to what you're looking for.

Before switching to another team, speaking with other parents can be a helpful way as well to find out about the culture and environment of the team and whether it may be a good fit. Parents are typically forthcoming about their experiences and this could help you in your decision-making process. Another key factor to consider before moving on from your current team or organization is what the goalie situation is with the new team. You want to make sure you ask the hard questions early such as expectations with regard to ice time. The more information you can get early the easier it will help you make the correct call.

Training

Training at the 10 to 13-year-old age bracket falls into the same pattern as the early years. Ideally, a goaltender receives goalie-specific training once a week during the season and attends a one-week summer camp. This does not mean that if you're going to do more in the summer they should stay away from training but one thing you don't want to do is overdo it too early at a young age, they should experience different sports and activities. If a goaltender is serious about their position, receiving position-specific training is essential. Training in the summertime starts to pick up and having a coach that connects with your son or daughter will be a big asset. You also get a good idea around this age as the players are starting to shoot the puck with a little bit more velocity and you'll be able to notice whether your goalie is a little puck shy or has no fear. If they start to trend toward being puck shy you may want to look at whether their equipment is doing a good job protecting them because it is typically goalies wearing inferior equipment that end up taking a few shots that make them begin to be more protective in nature.

Equipment

During the next step (ages 10 to 13) there will be some talk about organizations that provide equipment but it is quite likely that you will be on your own. At this point, you know what pieces of equipment need to be purchased but there will be a few decisions that you will have to make. One of the most important decisions that parents have to make when buying gear for their kids is the size. Often, parents think that bigger equipment will last longer because it'll give time so the kids grow into it. It may also seem that the bigger the equipment, the more protective it is.

As a longtime goalie coach, I can tell you quite emphatically how important it is for a goaltender to play with equipment that is appropriate in size as opposed to equipment that is too big. As a coach, we are trying to mold the goalie's muscle memory to learn the mechanics and techniques necessary for stopping pucks. Wanting the goalie to wear oversized equipment that becomes cumbersome on them, impacts their ability to move and therefore negatively affects building proper muscle memory. At the 10 to 13-year age level, having equipment that allows the goalie to move is essential for their long-term development.

The other impact that oversized equipment, particularly the pads, has on a goaltender is that it negatively impacts their skating. Skating is the cornerstone or the foundation of success between the pipes. If the pads are too big, skating will be inhibited and the goalie will have trouble skating from spot to spot and maintain their balance. There is one essential element when analyzing the size of a pad and that is the knee cradle. The knee cradle has what's called the landing pad and this is where the knee makes contact with the pad when the goalie drops. It is important that the knee lands squarely on the landing pad and not below or above it. This is truly how you know if the pad fits as opposed to using the eye test and looking straight at the goaltender. So, therefore, at the hockey store, your goalie should put their skates on, and the sales rep can stand behind the goalie and watch where the knee lands in the butterfly.

Another part of the pad sizing that you may want to consider is what's called the thigh rise. The thigh rise is the area of the pad that extends from the knee to the top of the pad itself. When you see a pad size followed by a + (Plus) sign the following number will note the additional thigh-rise as opposed to a standard pad. Therefore, if you are looking at a pair of pads that are noted as a 32 inches and compare it to a pad from the same manufacturer which is noted as a 32 + 1, what that means is that the knee cradle and landing pad will be the same in both pads but the +1 means there is an extra inch of height on this particular pad.

One thing you may want to consider at this age group is how quickly the kids grow, therefore, when you purchase your equipment is very important. You want to purchase that equipment either at the beginning of the summer which gives you time to get comfortable in the equipment or just before the start of the season. Don't be surprised if the new equipment only lasts for one season. Although it would be nice to buy equipment that is a little too big and would last longer, purchasing the equipment that fits properly will add to the experience of being a goaltender.

One system that has worked out well for some families is to have a relationship with another goalie family that has a child just a little bit older than yours. In this situation, the older goaltender passes down their equipment to the younger one which saves on some expense. Not always, but typically, equipment is built to last longer than just one season which normally is about all that the equipment will fit for. For some of the goalie families that I've been associated with the system has worked out very well and once again sometimes it's the association that arranges equipment.

The Break

As in the earlier years, a goalie should take at least eight weeks off during the year. Preferably, this is done in the spring and as mentioned in the last section it is important they are going to get away from the sights, sounds, and smells of the rink to maintain their enthusiasm and passion for the sport. What you were going to notice at the 10 to 13-year-age group is that spring and summer tournaments are picking up. You should never feel compelled to have to play during your son's or daughter's break time. It is not your responsibility to have them play in the spring or summer tournaments circuit just because someone needs a goalie.

If they are going to play in the spring and summer you may want to consider making sure your goalie gets some ice before the tournament. I find, particularly at this age, it is not easy to hop between the pipes after you haven't seen pucks for a long time. You may want to schedule lessons leading up to tournaments so your goalie has had the opportunity to feel some pucks and get their legs under them. Playing these tournaments is supposed to be fun but if a goalie doesn't play well it isn't too much fun. Therefore, if you are going to commit to playing a tournament, getting a few lessons and getting some ice time leading up to the tournament may be helpful.

Goalie Parent Interview #7: Vic DiPietro

Michael DiPietro is a 1999 born native of Windsor Ontario and is currently under contract with the Vancouver Canucks of the NHL. He was selected by the Canucks in the third round (64th overall) of the 2017 NHL Entry Draft. Prior to being drafted into the OHL, he played with the Sun County Panthers Minor Midget AAA team. As a junior Michael led his hometown Windsor Spitfires to the 2017 Memorial Cup Championship where he was named MVP and backstopped team Canada at the World Junior Championships. He was a member of the 2021 Canadian Men's World Championship team that captured gold.

When did your son decide to be a goalie?

Michael was like most other kids and played on a team that rotated players taking turns to play goalie. He was between the ages of 7 and 8 and after one game he just looked at me and said "I want to be a goalie." I could tell in the look of his eyes that this is what he really wanted to do and the very next year he was already playing on a AAA team.

What did you feel about that decision?

I was fine with it and as a former football player, I know how great it is to play a team sport. I was coaching back then and immediately started looking up drills and resources so I could help him. The one thing I did insist on is that he made the commitment in school and if he would hold up that end of the bargain I would support him in anything he chose to pursue. I then proceeded to be a typical dad and threw every great sports quote ever spoken at him!

What has been the best part of the journey so far?

The best part about being a goalie parent was the long drives on the 401. Michael's mother had passed so we had a lot of time to talk that through as well as a long list of other subjects including not making excuses or taking things too seriously. I feel truly blessed to have had that time with him and we are like best friends.

What has been the most challenging part of being a goalie parent?

The hardest thing about being a goalie parent was watching your son go through the valleys, especially when he was not home. You just hope that when they are not around that all the parental lessons you taught kick in and things will work out for the best. A great example of this was when Michael started his first NHL game at the age of 19. Although the game did not go as well as he would have liked I could not have been prouder on how he handled the media after the game. He knows what matters and it was at that moment he handled himself like a true professional.

What were the key aspects of his development that stand out to you?

When I look back at all the decisions that had to be made, I think one of the best was having him play lacrosse. He was already a baseball player but I also had him play lax in the summers. Playing other sports not only help them develop as an athlete but also reinforces that they are more than just a goalie. This really helped put things in perspective especially when you get asked to do so many hockey events, I believe playing other sports will make you more well-rounded than always just playing hockey.

Do you get nervous watching games and if so how do you combat those nerves?

When I am watching Michael play I really try to stay in the moment. I am not one to be on my phone or have conversations with other parents as I prefer just to focus on the game and watch my son play. Now, it's a whole different story for my wife! I watch the game and while everything is happening I just quietly wish the game goes well.

What is one piece of advice you would give other goalie parents?

In my experience, one of the most important things a parent can do is let the child come to you with where they want to focus their energy. It really comes down to the passion of the athlete that will determine how far they will go. Once they have charted a path all you can do is support them. It's important to find them the right resources and coaching. Michael was fortunate to have so many good goalie coaches throughout his development which is another key element. Being surrounded by good people is a big reason why some kids make it.

The Middle Years (14-to-17) High School and Midget

The middle years are when things start to get interesting for goaltenders who are motivated to see how far they could go with the position and the sport. As the USA Hockey study determined, a hockey player's optimal window of trainability is between 13 and 15 years of age. If you were not one to provide a lot of training early on it is important that you don't miss the window available in this age bracket. The reason why the 13 to 15 years of age bracket is so productive for development is that the goalies are typically strong enough to do all the moves that they're being taught, have an understanding of what training is all about, and why they want to get better as goalies but they are not quite old enough to be too cool for school when it comes to being taught how to play the position.

How Do You Know?

Entering the 14 to 17-year-old age bracket goalies still can play recreationally but it is during this period that the competition level makes a big jump. In North America, this is the time where the kids enter high school and some will now play for a public or private high school or continue with their club program. High school may consist of 4 age groups and club programs may move from 1 to 2 year age brackets. Club programs start aiming to qualify for national championships and in Canada, the CHL draft for major junior teams is right around the corner. Obviously, the stakes start to get higher during this time. And it is important to have a discussion with your son or daughter at the beginning of this stage to see what their aspirations are.

This time is about knowing what the end game is and doing what is essential to have a chance to get there. This means research, tryouts, comparisons, and challenges. Going through this is necessary to be successful and will include some ups and downs but what I am encouraging is that before this stage starts both you and your goalie are on the same page and working towards the same goal. As a parent myself, I always said that I would support whatever my kids wanted to do and help them chase their dreams but I always wanted to make sure that this is what they wanted and not influenced by me. After deciding the course with your son or daughter you may want to continue to have the occasional check-in conversation to make sure that their goals and aspirations are the same as when they started so you can support them in the best manner possible.

Where To Play?

Depending on what country you are in there may be more decisions than you can shake a stick at the 14 to 17-year-age bracket. You may have the opportunity to play in a hockey academy, a prep school, a public school or continue down the club path. The same rules apply with regard to picking the right program and that is the situation... playing in a competitive environment and gaining experience.

In choosing an academy or school, if there is an older, stronger goalie that is ahead of them, your son and daughter may miss valuable development time as they wait their turn to take the starting job. One of the dilemmas we have in my region is that most of the kids move from club hockey, where they play inside their age group, and move into a school environment where they're competing against kids that are four years older. Often a strong goaltender who had played a lot of games leading into their school experience find themselves just sitting on the bench or the JV team. One thing is for certain, it is difficult to progress when you are not playing many games. When parents are looking at a school environment it is important to know what the plan is and when your son or daughter is expected to be playing.

Despite what a coach will tell you about what the projected ice time is going to be at the academy or school level, it is still up to the goaltender to play at the level that the coach projected to earn the net and valuable ice time. When considering the academy or school option you may want to inquire about goalie coaching but this may not be something they provide. Although intuitively, it would seem a priority for a goalie to want to make sure that they have a high level of goalie coaching during the season, in my experience it is most important to get the necessary training in the summertime and therefore, what the school provides for goalie training is not necessarily a deal-breaker for me.

If you are choosing a club program as opposed to a school the questions remain the same for the coach to understand what the expectations are going to be for the season. There is not a one-size-fits-all when it comes to whether to go to an academy, private school, or club program. It comes down to the right fit for your son or daughter and it is the parents' responsibility to figure out what the lineage of the school team is so you can make an educated decision on whether that is the right fit. If you are stuck between options, the "go where your wanted" mantra may help to be a deciding factor.

Making The Team

The big difference for a goalie playing in the 14 to 17-year-age bracket is that the process of making the team never seems to stop. With recruiting, goalies, and players switching teams at a high rate in this age bracket, a goalie never has to stop proving themselves and in my mind, they are always trying to make the team whether they have a spot or not. Having to prove yourself regardless of what you've done in the past is just the world that goalies live in. Therefore, every time a goalie steps on the ice for practice or a game, they should not take their spot for granted and continually do what they have to do to be successful.

In this age bracket, CHL and college recruiters are closely monitoring players. When picking a team you may want to consider the type of exposure to the scouts and recruiters that that team offers. It may seem daunting for an inexperienced hockey parent but by the time you get to this level a goalie parent has a good idea of the stronger programs and schools available. There are not a lot of stones unturned when it comes to scouting and recruiting but being on a higher profile team and league at this age group can be beneficial. It will always come down to how a goalie performs over a long period of time. By playing for a team that attracts scouts and recruiters you can put your goalie in a better situation and a chance to show what they can do.

Tournament Teams

Once a goalie gets to the 14 to 17-year-old age group off-season tournaments become the norm. They become more than just gaining experience as there is an emphasis on exposure. Whether that exposure comes in the form of colleges, junior teams, prep schools, and academies, playing in the summertime becomes an integral part of the recruiting and scouting process. Because of this, choosing spring and summer tournaments typically revolves around how many scouts and from where typically attend the showcases.

One of the best pieces of advice I have ever heard comes from Quinnipiac University's head hockey coach Rand Pecknold. Several years ago, Rand attended a Stop It Goaltending event and spoke to our goalies about the recruiting process. He made a statement that I'll never forget. He said that more players lose scholarships in the summertime at the tournaments than actually gain them. It was quite a strong statement and a real eye-opener for all the goalies in attendance.

What coach Pecknold had time to explain was that there were so many summer tournaments that there were players that were playing too much hockey as they tried to get as much exposure as they could in a short period of time. What he found was that because the players were playing so much they were not playing at the same intensity level that they would play at during the regular season. Because of this lack of intensity, it actually produced a negative viewing for the coaches in the fact that the players did not perform at a level that they were capable of. Therefore, the message is clear... goalies should pick a limited amount of tournaments but prepare for those tournaments and compete as hard as they can.

One interesting note about the elite tournament circuit at this age group is that at this point they are now a mixture of kids from all sorts of different areas. What happened is that in the 10 to the 13-year-old age group the elite tournament circuit coaches start to get to know all the players from the different teams and slowly but surely begin to recruit players from other teams. By the time you get to the 14 to 17-year-old age group a lot of teams are mixed. Since the elite teams only meet at the hockey hubs and do not practice, the players can play for any team they choose and there are no rules regarding recruiting all the teams' players. This circuit is very good and very competitive and it's something to consider for the right goalie.

It is typically at 14 years old that national teams across the world start their national development camps and evaluation process. Typically, if a goalie has an opportunity to participate in any of the camps or tryouts situations for the national program this is a "must-do." Anytime you are involved with a national team tryout or tournament it is an opportunity not only to test yourself against the best and grow as a goaltender but also gain the best exposure potential for scouts and recruiters. As a goalie parent, it is important to learn about your country's national development program so you don't miss out on when and where the tryouts take place and as regions and countries are different you may want to keep track of any changes and how things are done if your goalie is very strong at their age level.

Tryouts

Tryouts are definitely the norm in this age bracket but there are also some nuances to the tryout circuit that may not have been at an earlier level. Teams will often have players and goalies practice with their team before the actual tryouts. If you are a parent looking for opportunities for your son or daughter it may be worth your while to ask the coach if they can get on the ice with the team at practice during the second half of the season. This will give the coach an exclusive viewing of your son or daughter. I'm a big proponent of this system because it allows the coach to see the goalie with all of their existing players and how they compare to the goalies that are currently with the club. Not every organization does this but it often results in a quality viewing and possibly being offered a spot before tryouts actually take place.

Next Year

Typically in the 14 to 17-year-old age bracket goalies tend to stay for multiple years. Making a school or academy commitment traditionally means anywhere from two to four years. Club programs are typically set with their goaltenders once they get to this stage. When looking at the academy or the private school route you may find that if you wait till January most likely at the youth hockey level, you will be too late to the party. Typically, recruiting takes place in the fall and a lot of the goalies know where they're heading by the time the winter holidays roll around. The one thing that I would recommend in this age bracket is to put together a website with your goalie's contact information, hockey history as well as their schedule and videos.

A goalie that has their own website has control of what people are seeing about them. I like to explain to goalies that they are just like a company as they are a brand. The beauty of having a site is that you can update it on demand. I recommend posting game videos no more than three minutes in length. Parents can record game action and the kids can put their clips together and post it on the site. I know as a coach, the last thing I want to do is sit for two hours watching a game with 24 shots against. A pre-cut game of 24 shots in clips will only take a few minutes to go through. With everyone so concerned with how little time they have, keeping the video short will increase your likelihood that a coach will watch it.

Training

In-season training at the 14 to 17-year-old level may look a little bit different than in previous years. If a goaltender continues with their club program you may find that the number of practices has increased to three or four times a week. With that much time on the ice, the schedule may not allow for as much goalie-specific training independently. If a goaltender is playing for their school they may be in the same practice situation and on the ice five or six times a week. A decision that's faced by goalies and their parents is how to properly provide the goalie-specific training necessary to keep improving.

Performance at the 14 to 17-year-old level will dictate a goalie's opportunities to continue to move forward and end up advancing from one level to the next. If a goaltender is with a club or school where they are on the ice five to six times per week it is hard to add additional training on top of the schedule they already have. The impact of doing this is that they may get halfway through the season and start to experience diminishing returns. If the goaltender has time to continue with a weekly specific lesson, this is an ideal situation but if a goalie does not have the time then you may have to go through periods without this type of training. The one caveat to this is if the goaltender is on a team where they are not the starter. If a goaltender is not the starter and has a full practice schedule they are not actually playing the games and therefore, to keep up, adding goalie-specific training on top of their busy schedule is definitely something to consider.

Because of the number of practices and the performance aspect of this stage in development, summer training takes on greater importance. As opposed to training a week at a time as when the goalies were younger they will typically need a summer-long program to work on the areas of their game that need improvement. There's simply not enough time in a one-week program to provide the training necessary to remain competitive in this age group. At Stop It Goaltending our summer programs typically last for 8 weeks in duration, with the training sessions lasting 80 minutes and are conducted twice per week.

In addition to a summer-long training program goaltenders that have the ambition to continue moving forward typically participate in off-ice training programs. In most areas around the world, there are training programs specifically designed for athletes and done in an environment that pushes everyone to get the most out of their workouts. Although it would be ideal to have an off-ice program specifically designed for goaltenders this may not always be the case. Most off-ice programs at a reputable athletic training facility should be able to fit most of your needs. Like finding a goalie coach, finding an athletic training center that will be a good fit for your son or daughter may take some leg work and may require asking some older goalies what they do and where they train, but in the end, it will be well worth it.

One training that is available for goalies who are interested in pursuing the college route is in the form of summer camps that are put on by the colleges themselves. US colleges and universities typically run these camps to make additional income, attract potential student-athletes to their campuses and get a chance to evaluate the players on and off the ice. Typically what you'll see is relatively the same group of assistant coaches from different colleges and universities assisting each other. Therefore, if you go to one of the college summer hockey camps you will find there are plenty of coaches that are on the staff that also coach at other colleges or universities. Attending one of these summer camps is a benefit for a goalie because not only do the coaches get a chance to see them play in practice but they get to know them as people and start to build a relationship. You may have to decide between doing the summer camps and tournaments or ideally have a mix of both.

Equipment

If you remember earlier in the book, I mentioned how affordable goalie equipment could be at the younger levels. Unfortunately, that isn't the case in the 14 to 17-year-old bracket. The prices will increase so therefore, your choices will have to be well thought out. Although customization is something more prevalent for the next level you will find that there may be more choices to be made. One of the key aspects to keep in mind when purchasing equipment at this age group is that the equipment fits and is the right style for your goaltender. With different equipment manufacturers, you will find different strengths and weaknesses. A goaltender's game can dramatically change based on the style of equipment they are wearing.

If you want to know the most common mistake made in this age group by the goalies and their parents it is buying equipment because the goalie's favorite goalie wears a particular brand or style. The equipment the NHL stars are wearing may be great for them but it may not be the best for your goalie. Because the equipment is such a big part of why kids choose to play goalie a lot of them become what is affectionately referred to in the business as gearheads. Gearheads are people that know all the specs that go along with all the different choices in equipment and are very knowledgeable. You or your child do not have to be a gearhead but particularly at this level, it is great to have someone at a hockey shop that understands goalie equipment and can properly fit and size your goalie in the equipment based on how they play.

There is much made of the design and color scheme on equipment. Over the past five years, there has been a dramatic increase in all-white gear. Goalies like all white because that way they can play on any team and their equipment will match the jerseys. If your son or daughter is expected to play for several different teams during the season you may want to consider going all white. If your goalie is going to be with the program or a school over a prolonged period this is a great opportunity to get equipment with the color scheme of the team or the school. Because it is difficult for hockey shops to carry a lot of different combinations of colors, you may have to order the colors and the designs either online or with a hockey shop.

Typically at this age level, equipment is bought at the completion of the season primarily because of the time needed to obtain the equipment and that most goalies would like to use the equipment during summer training to get comfortable with it before the next season starts. I can remember the day it used to take a long time to break in equipment but this is no longer the case. It always amazes me how quickly a goaltender can pull equipment out of a box and get it ready for game time. That being said, having new equipment for the summer will allow them to practice with their new gear building confidence and control leading into the season.

The Break

The break for the 14 to the 17-year-old age group is perhaps the trickiest of all levels. For me, the goal of every goaltender is to take 8 weeks away from the ice to allow the body and the mind to rest up, ideally, it is done in the spring. The issue with this is that there are now so many hockey events in the spring that it makes it difficult for a goaltender to find time to rest. With tryouts for some of the higher-level programs you simply cannot be off the ice and expect to perform well at tryout time and therefore you'll need some lead-up time. Also with so many exposure tournaments available in the spring and summer, it may be impossible to put 8 weeks together.

If because of tryouts and tournaments an 8-week break between the end of the previous season and the start of the next season may not be possible, you may want to consider breaking up the weeks into smaller segments. Therefore, instead of 8 consecutive weeks, maybe 2 separate 4-week breaks will fit in the schedule. Regardless of how you break up the weeks, you should look for opportunities to string weeks together. You may want to spend a little bit of extra time in advance looking at what the schedule is going to be so that you don't miss opportunities to take that time off the ice.

Goalie Parent Interview #8: Shelley Woll

Raised in the suburbs of St. Louis, Joseph Woll has excelled both internationally and in college and is currently under contract with the Toronto Maple Leafs of the National Hockey League. Joe was selected in the third round and 62nd overall at the 2016 NHL draft and played for the St Louis AAA Blues before heading to the US National Development Program. At the U18 World Championship, he led all goaltenders statistically and won both a gold and bronze medal at the World Junior Championships. At Boston College, he was a member of the All Rookie team, team MVP and a Hobey Baker Award candidate.

When did your son decide to be a goalie?

Joseph started out playing both goalie and player but he always volunteered to be the goalie any chance he had. One spring we received a postcard in the mail advertising a tryout for a spring tournament team to be made up of the best kids in the area. On the postcard, you had to select forward, defense, or goalie and Joseph wanted to try out as a goalie. The concern was that he was going to try out against other kids that were full-time goalies and he didn't have much experience. He also didn't have his own equipment so we had to piece together enough gear for the tryout. We told him if he made the team we would set him up with gear and he was selected as an alternate. Another player that was on the tournament team was Trent Frederic now of the Boston Bruins. Trent was a player/goalie at that time and when he could not go to a tournament because of a first communion Joseph stepped in and led the squad to a championship in of all places Toronto. From that point forward there was no looking back.

What did you feel about that decision?

When Joseph decided to be a goalie we had no understanding of the stress, the highs and lows, and the cost associated with the position. All I saw was a boy that smiled from ear to ear when he played goalie. I never thought about what the journey was going to be like and didn't even think about the 90 miles an hour or slap shots that were eventually going to be shot at my son. All I knew was how much he loved being a goalie and our job as parents is to support that passion.

What has been the best part of the journey so far?

The journey has been unbelievable and the thing that really stands out is the travel. Having the opportunity to travel and see new places and visit cities that we never would have gone to has been great. The most important part of travel is the time that you spend as a family and when you look back you realize that those moments on the road or in the hotel are the best of times. More important than the travel is watching your child find what they love from the depths of their being and willing to put in the work necessary to be successful at it.

What has been the most challenging part of being a goalie parent?

It always seems as if the highs and lows are higher and lower for a goalie. It's not always easy to watch your son go through the ups and downs but it is essential for their development. As hard as it may be for a parent to try to put a band-aid on struggles that happen, it would be a disservice not to let them go through it and figure out how to move forward. I know it seems counterintuitive because all we want to do as parents is to protect our kids but we have to have faith and understand that adversity builds confidence. If we shield them from this, we will take away their growth as people and athletes.

What were the key aspects of his development that stand out to you?

There were really two aspects of development that had a dramatic impact on Joseph's career. The first being finding a goalie school in the area led by Bruce Racine. Being part of Bruce's goalie school was being part of a community of mentors, coaches, and fellow goalies who are passionate about the position and were there for each other. Joseph would beg to go to goalie training and would never ever let us miss a session. He has been so fortunate to have so many great coaches from Bruce to Kevin Rieter, Mike Ayers of Boston College, and now the goalie coaches in Toronto.

Do you get nervous watching games and if so how do you combat those nerves?

I've never been one to sit down while watching Joseph and I prefer to stand. You may find me high in the rafters watching the game and I love watching warm-up as well. I know what is in his heart and I just want the world to see that. I have confidence that he will do well because he works so hard and is so dedicated. The lessons are hard to watch but you just have to know that that is part of the learning process and if all else fails... a glass of wine isn't the worst idea!

What is one piece of advice you would give other goalie parents?

If I could get one piece of advice to other goalie parents it would be to enjoy the journey. Hockey is truly a tremendous sport with a culture that is second to none. The fondest memories that I have are the early morning practices, getting up before the sun with muffins, bananas, and hot chocolate, and then watching the sunrise as we crossed the bridge heading towards the rink. In the hockey journey, it is truly the small things that are actually the big things at the end of the day and I hope that all goalie parents can enjoy the journey while it happens.

The Junior Years (18-20 years of age) Junior

Before we address anything in this section, I first have to say if you are reading this with a goalie that is still playing hockey... congratulations. Although it may not feel like it at the time your goalie is one of the few kids that are still playing at this point. Making it to the junior age group is not easy to do so I hope you take the opportunity to congratulate your goalie and while you're at it yourself. Junior hockey is perhaps the most difficult level to play at. Success or failure at the junior level will dictate if this is the end of the road or you can move on to the next step. The goaltending position level is intense because of the pyramid effect. There just aren't nearly enough nets for all the good goaltenders that are out there that want to keep playing.

If you are in Europe and have been with the same club for junior hockey, then you will see a lot more movement than what you've seen in the past and a home-bred goalie may be challenged as other goalies come in from outside the area. As mentioned earlier a goalie will never stop having to prove themselves and even if they have been with the organization throughout their youth hockey career they must be prepared that there will be challenges and they must be ready to meet them head-on. For a female in this age group, it will be time to move on to college or university although there are increasingly more junior hockey opportunities for girls. I will be talking about some nuances of playing at the college level while we discuss the next level so for now, we'll save our discussion to the junior ranks.

How Do You Know?

How do you know if your goalie is cut out for junior hockey and this is the best thing for them to do? Kids often have to choose between entering college and playing junior hockey. There's a growing trend for the colleges to take older more experienced goaltenders and therefore student-athletes are entering the college ranks at 21 years of age. In Canada, players have to decide whether to enter the CHL and play major junior or play junior "A" hockey to obtain a scholarship. Regardless of the path, junior hockey is about playing to win and the better you play the more you'll develop. If you enter this system you must be all in because if you have one foot in the door and one foot out it will make it exponentially harder to be successful. If your goalie plays junior hockey, have one thing in mind and that's to move to the next level. If that is the goal of your goalie then junior hockey is a level that must be conquered.

Tryouts

Tryouts at the junior hockey level in North America come in many shapes and sizes. A lot of times, goalies will go to tryouts even though the team already knows exactly who they are going to select. Some people may consider it a waste of time for a goalie to go to a tryout when the team already knows whom they like but the issue is it is hard to know this in advance. Doing your homework and asking the right questions may help alleviate some of these issues and save some time and money. Junior teams in the CHL have a draft as well as the USHL and the NAHL in the US. The USHL and the NAHL have what's called pre-draft camps, followed by main camps, followed by the actual training camp at the beginning of the season. In the New England area where the NCDC league is prevalent, they hold tryouts in the spring and have exposure tournaments throughout the summer where they continue to evaluate potential players.

To be able to go over all the different options and scenarios of tryouts at the junior level would possibly take up a book in itself. The one thing you have to keep in mind is that teams are trying to find goalies that are going to help them win and if the goalies do not get the job done at the junior hockey level teams are quick to make a change and find an alternative. You would think that this pressure would be bad for the goaltender as it would be very discouraging to be put under pressure so often but this is actually where you see development. To play hockey at the college and pro level is not easy and that is where the kids want to end up. It is the challenges that they face at the junior level which will give them the mental toughness to allow them to succeed as they move on.

Major junior hockey in Canada is free for players as well as some of the junior "A" programs and leagues but there seems to be a trend in charging Canadian players to play at the lower junior level. Junior hockey in the States can either be subsidized by the club, a pay-to-play system, or a hybrid of the two. It is important to educate yourself when you get to the junior level to what options are available and what the expectations are, financially. Finances are important because going to the different tryout camps can really add up. If you add up the cost of the camp, the travel to get to the camp, the hotel room and meals, one tryout camp that has a sticker price of let's say $350 may end up actually costing you $1000 and those dollars can add up quickly.

Where To Play?

Deciding where to play at the 18 to 20-year-old level has a lot to do with the level of the goalie and the opportunity that they may have. For European goalies, the way that the clubs are organized they will move up to the organization's junior team, and if they have a lower-level professional team they may even have the opportunity to play for that team. North American goalies typically come down to a choice between playing CHL Major Junior Hockey or Junior A/ Tier 1, Tier II or Tier III. The goalies in Canada may opt not to play Major Junior hockey to pursue a US college scholarship whereas a US-born goaltender may opt to play a Major Junior Hockey in lieu of pursuing the college route.

As noted in the section before there's a growing trend for US colleges and universities to recruit older goaltenders. It is not uncommon to find 21-year-old freshman goalies on college rosters. Goalies that have moved on to the CHL are controlled by the team that owns their rights while players that are not pursuing the CHL route are free to choose a team to play for. Up until this point, I have been pretty adamant in my recommendation to find a competitive team where the goalies are going to get a lot of shots regardless of whether the team is a powerhouse or not. There is still value to that type of team at this level as a goalie really gets a chance to show what they can do and be an impact player. This is an opportunity for a goalie to get noticed as they are a difference-maker.

Playing for a powerhouse team at this age bracket has its advantages as well. Because this is scouting and recruiting time, playing for a strong team will most likely result in impressive statistical numbers and the goalie that has good skill and good numbers increases their probability to get scouted and recruited. Playing on one of these teams goalies may see fewer shots and less action but the flip side is that the scout that is evaluating the goalie also has statistics to back up what their eyes are seeing. Once again there is no one-size-fits-all for all goalies but if you are in a situation to play for a team that has a chance to win a championship this also means a high probability of making the playoffs and playing meaningful games in front of evaluators.

The NHL draft is held during this time and typically takes place at the end of June. To be eligible for the NHL draft North American players are between the ages of 18 and 20 but there is a fourth year of eligibility for Europeans as well. The majority of drafted players are in their first year of eligibility but you can also get drafted after that first year. My son Joey was ranked by Central Scouting as the 14th best goalie in North America his first year and was not drafted but was ranked #10 in the preceding year and was selected in the seventh round by the Ottawa Senators.

In this day and age, there are very few players who are goaltenders that slip through the cracks from getting evaluated by the NHL teams. Scouts have access to two incredible video platforms where they'll be able to see every shot of every game of a drafted goaltender including every win, loss, and goal against. Playing for any of the key leagues throughout North America and Europe will guarantee exposure to the NHL teams and scouts. There is much debate on which league is the best to play for but there are way too many variables that a goalie parent can't control. The best bet is to find a situation that fits best for your goalie and then simply... play well.

Although there are junior leagues for women, typically female student-athletes that play hockey start their university between the ages of 18 and 20. With that being said the recruiting of potential NCAA players and goalies begin in their sophomore year of high school but there is the opportunity for a goaltender that may have developed late to earn scholarships at this time. Therefore, this is a period of performance during the season, and additional development is added in the off-season.

Tournaments

There are tournaments at the 18 to 20-year-old age level but a lot of these tournaments now take the shape of tryout camps. Although there are still some great at large type tournaments to go to, you'll find that a lot of the tournament teams are actually junior organizations that are using tournaments to evaluate players or the actual tryout is in a tournament format.

Tryouts

Tryouts for junior teams take place throughout the spring and summer and most also have a training camp to start the season. Each league and each organization can differ on how they do things. Regardless of when the tryouts are or the format there is just one thing to remember when it comes to trying out at this level... tryouts are a way to identify the goalies and who will be invited to training camp. Making a team in the spring or summer tryout format does not guarantee that the goalie will be with the team when they drop the puck to start the season. Advancing past the tryout is merely another opportunity to prove yourself.

Without going through every league and country in the world I will use the United States Hockey League (USHL) and the North American Hockey League (NAHL) as an example of this. A USHL team will start the season with their training camp, typically at the end of August, and will carry at least three goalies at this time. An NAHL team will start their training camp at the same time and their training camp roster will typically consist of at least three goaltenders. Therefore, regardless of if you are at a USHL or an NAHL training camp, you are looking to earn one of the two spots available. When the season is going to start at the USHL level they are only allowed to carry two of the three goalies they had in training camp and therefore one of the goalies has to get cut. The North American League team has to do the same thing and submit two goalies for their opening day roster and cut any additional goaltenders that were at training camp. Where it gets interesting is that when a goalie gets cut from the USHL team they need a place to play which is often the NAHL. Therefore, the NAHL team that's selected two goalies to start the season now will have to cut one of their goalies to make room for the newly acquired USHL cut. So, therefore, of the three-plus goalies starting the season's training camp in the North American Hockey

League only one may be left once the USHL gets underway and makes their cuts. This is merely an example that regardless of what team a goalie made in tryout camp, a goaltender at the junior level must always continue to perform to retain their position on the team.

Next Year

During the junior years, next year could mean anywhere from going to the NHL to being out of hockey altogether. An American or Canadian player that plays junior "A" hockey and is not returning is traditionally looking to start their university. Where to go to university, the cardinal rule will still apply and that is... go where you wanted.

A junior player in Canada is either heading to the pros or the CHL and Canadian university. Just because a player was drafted at 18 it doesn't mean by the time that junior is over that they will be signed to an entry-level contract. Typically, a CHL player that does not sign professionally continues to play hockey and to go to university in Canada. Because the NCAA, which is the governing body of university athletics in the USA, considers major junior hockey to be professional, a Canadian player cannot attend an American college or university without sitting out a minimum of one year, and typically the number of games played in the CHL in addition. A European goalie will either stay with their club or move on to another club or possibly head to North America.

Regardless of what country your goalie plays in, the fact is that for them to progress it's going to require them to play well at the level they are at. The goalie pyramid starts to get very tight at this point and there are not nearly enough nets to satisfy the demand of the goalies interested in playing.

Training

When you get to the junior level there is very little opportunity during the course of the season to receive goalie-specific training away from the team. Most teams provide a goalie coach and therefore, the goalies work with their assigned coach with the emphasis being on performance. During the junior years, there's a lot of emphasis on the wins and the losses, summertime becomes a pivotal time to work on deficiencies in your goalie's game and simply... get better.

Once you get to the 18 to 20-year-old age bracket when it comes to training, there's no messing around. At this point, the goalies understand the importance of training and how an off-season can dramatically affect their performance level during the season. Most goalies have their goalie coach at this point but because of where they are slated to play and who the coaches are for that team, they may want to consider training with their performance coach as opposed to the development coach that they have had since they were kids.

Not only is on-ice training in the summertime pivotal, adding strength and conditioning in the weight room is essential as well. Some goalies will work out at an athletic performance center often looking for extra training such as yoga, vision training, mindfulness, and cognitive training as well. Anything that can help the goalie improve their game is something that most goalies are willing to try.

There are five things that goalies must keep in mind when it comes to summer training. As a goalie parent, this list might be worth reviewing before training begins.

1. Have a plan.

Goalies should have a clear-cut plan for what they want to work on in the summertime based on their experiences throughout the season.

2. Warm-up.

When getting to the rink in the summertime a goalie must have a good warm-up before getting on the ice. This warm-up will help set up a productive workout.

3. Ask questions.

Goalies shouldn't just complete drills without understanding why they are doing them. It's important to know the situation in the application of the drill. Goalies should feel comfortable asking their instructor about its application.

4. Mix it up.

One of the best learning experiences in summer camps is the opportunity to train with other goalies. Working with other goalies allows you to see variations of mechanics and strategies.

5. Be present.

Blocking out distractions and staying focused during games and having the ability to get into the zone is equally important to practice. Use the motto "be where your feet are". This means that regardless of what happened before the training session or what's going to happen after the training session, the goal is to focus on the session itself.

Equipment

If you've gotten to this level you know that the cost of equipment has risen dramatically with the age of the goaltender. I wish I could tell you it's going to stop, unfortunately, I can't. Hopefully, your goalies' junior team can help with the cost of the equipment but you may find as a goalie parent that at this age the goalies are fully aware of customization and the ability to get variations to their equipment that may not be the standard or out of the box. The one thing that you need to know about ordering custom equipment is that it typically takes 8 to 12 weeks to get your order. What this means is you should really be looking at placing your order after the season so that the goalies get their gear in time to get used to it during their summer training.

The Break

The junior level is no different from any other level where taking eight weeks off the ice is the goal but it can be problematic depending on if there are tryouts to attend. If all goes well and a goalie doesn't have to report to any spring or summer camps, like for colleges, you can actually stretch eight weeks into twelve depending on how things go. Typically, a goaltender would like to get at least eight weeks of rest and eight weeks of training before they start their team's training camp with a minimum lead time of four to six weeks. Break time should consist of getting a mental break from the game and therefore, clearing the mind. This means doing other things such as golf and hiking. Getting outdoors is an awesome way to re-center and when it's time to get back on the ice you want to make sure that goalies get excited again.

Goalie Parent Interview #9: Claire Desbiens

Ann-Renée Desbiens is a 1994 born goaltender, is the national team goalie for Team Canada and notched a silver medal at the 2018 Winter Olympics. After playing for the Beaubourg Seigneurs Midget AA team she went to star at the University of Wisconsin in the NCAA where she led the team to four Frozen Four appearances. At Wisconsin, she won the coveted Patty Kazmaier Award as the nation's top player. Ann-Renee also represented her country at the Women's World Championships in 2015 winning the silver medal. Born in La Malbaie, QC, CAN, Ann-Renée played youth hockey for AHM Charlevoix and most recently she participated in the women's ice hockey showcase at the 2020 NHL All-Star Game.

When did your daughter decide to be a goalie?

Ann-Renée loved being a goalie at home with her brothers and sister so when she had a chance to be a goalie on a real team, she jumped at the opportunity. At that time there was a lack of goalies at the novice level and one of our friends was coaching. We told her if you want it, then to go for it and since then she has always known where she belongs... on the ice and in the net.

What did you feel about that decision?

My husband and I were very happy about Ann-Renée's decision to be a goalie while being nervous at the same time because we knew very well that the goaltender is a very important position on the team. However, throughout the years, we have known that she had made the right decision because every time she played in net she was full of life. She has made us very proud of the person she has become today.

What has been the best part of the journey so far?

We realize that as parents all our efforts and sacrifices are greatly rewarded and we are full of pride every time we look at her. Meeting other passionate parents has been a big part of enjoying this journey as we have made a lot of new friends. As of today, living the Olympic dream has been the best reward so far.

What has been the most challenging part of being a goalie parent?

The disappointment and the tears of your child after a game can be very difficult because you have to give them a lot of support and comfort to be able to continue to face the challenges of being a goalie. As parents, it is especially hard to hear some of the comments of other people who attend the games. The goalie can be the hero at one point but as soon as the puck sneaks past the goalie and is in the net...some people seem to forget about all the beautiful saves made before that. Also, the refusal of certain teams to take your child because of the different gender hurt us a lot, but fortunately Ann-Renée was able to persevere and prove them wrong. Despite some setbacks she was able to continuously improve through effort and determination and those small victories eventually turned into giant steps.

What were the key aspects of her development that stand out to you?

Courage and determination are the two words that sum up the key to Ann-Renée's development. The desire to prove that our little girl's dream can come true and that we have to really believe in it. She had the will to overcome the trials and tribulations and not give up on her dreams. The autonomy she has had has allowed her to move forward in life and above all develop the ability to find a solution and something positive to all the challenges a goalie faces along the way.

Do you get nervous watching games and if so, how do you combat those nerves?

Yes, we are nervous, but I don't think there is much we can do to change it. That's just part of the game. Sometimes I close my eyes for a few seconds, take a little walk in the arena, and even find myself trying to do some exercises while sitting... in the end, I don't know how much that helps decrease my stress level but I try.

What is one piece of advice you would give other goalie parents?

We do not regret anything about our journey as parents of a goaltender. One piece of advice I could offer other parents is not to be too hard on your child. The best approach is to encourage them not to let go because of setbacks but rather persevere, it is well worth it. Your child's experiences on and off the ice will fuel your families evenings and will be etched forever in your memories. Your presence and your encouragement to your child will become a source of motivation and comfort. Simply unforgettable and wonderful moments.

College or Pro (20 and older) College and Professional

Once you get to the college and pro level you may find it hard to believe but goalie's parents aren't that much different. A lot of the same issues older goalies face during this period is not that much different as when they were kids. I vividly remember a phone call with Rich Schneider, the father of Cory Schneider where we talked about some of the issues Cory was facing at the time in the NHL. I'll never forget hanging up the phone and saying to myself... that was virtually the same conversation that I typically have with a parent of a youth hockey goalie. Now that I have a son that has gone through all the levels I can experience this for myself as well. It is not a lot different than when he was younger.

When I first started coaching in the NHL with the Boston Bruins, I had a similar experience as a coach. When I would be listening to what the NHL coaches were telling the players I would chuckle to myself that these are the same things that youth hockey coaches tell their kids all the time. "Get pucks deep", "protect the puck", "get in front of the goalie", "finish your checks" and so on. The foundation of good solid hockey doesn't change from peewees to pros and players have to be reminded of the same thing. For a goalie parent, you would be amazed by the conversations you have with your 20-year old that they are not that much different than what you had when they were 10.

The one thing you have to remember when your son or daughter makes it to the college or pro level is what we talked about at the very beginning of this book when they were a young boy or girl just getting started. We discussed where to sit while watching the games so that they would know you are there, whether they played great or struggled and you would support them. No one expects the goalie parent to have all the answers for their goalie but the one thing that we can all do is listen and let the kids talk things through and just be there. As far as parents' emotions, things aren't going to change. We feel the same way when we watch our kids as adults as we do when they're just getting going.

Goalie Parent Interview #10: Kristine Costello-Avron

Collin Delia, an undrafted 1994 born goalie from Rancho Cucamonga and Glendora, California, rose through the goalie ranks and is currently under contract with the Chicago Blackhawks of the NHL. Playing for both the California Titans 18U AAA and Orange County HC 18U AAA, he progressed on to win a Robertson Cup in the North American Hockey League for the Amarillo Bulls. Collin was signed by the Blackhawks after a stellar junior season at Merrimack College where he was awarded the 2016-2017 Hockey East Goaltender of the Year. As successful of a player he is on the ice, his off-ice accomplishments stand out as he won the NAHL Community Service Award as well as the Rockford IceHogs Man of the year.

When did your son decide to be a goalie?

Collin started playing goalie when he was very young, about 4-years old. At first, they used a shooter tutor in the net but as soon as the teams had goalies the coach rotated the kids. He said he wanted to try it out and loved it so much that he wanted to be a full-time goalie ever since. Once he took over the position that's all he wanted to play, so much so that he preferred hockey to any other sport. He played T-ball, for one season, but quickly went back to hockey. He found his passion early.

What did you feel about that decision?

Being that we lived in California, I personally had little experience with hockey other than taking figure skating lessons when I was a kid at the LA Kings practice facility. When Collin first started playing, we weren't worried about injuries because the kids were so small, too, we were naive at the time of what the commitment and the cost of being a goaltender was. Youth ice hockey is different in California, as opposed to on the East Coast, where it seems like each town has its own rink. It didn't take long to figure out that there was going to be a lot of travel and the costs associated with playing, equipment, and private lessons/training were going to add up. That being said, seeing how much he enjoyed it, we were going to make it work for him, no matter what. Collin also showed his commitment by always completing his schoolwork so that he could travel to and from tournaments both out-of-state and in Canada.

What has been the best part of the journey so far?

The best part of being a goalie parent was what happened on those long car-rides and flights. We traveled to San Jose, Arizona, Nevada, Illinois, Florida, and Canada for tournaments. I don't know about how it is in other sports but in hockey, the travel is such a commitment while at the same time the best part because the conversations went far beyond hockey and sports and we were able to talk a lot about life. Perspective is so important and now when I see Collin with his fiancé and baby, and see how he has matured, I am very proud. I think that those hours spent together have contributed in a positive way, not only to who he is as a hockey player, but to his development as a person.

What has been the most challenging part of being a goalie parent?

The quickest thing that comes to mind is how hard it was to watch him take the blame for losses. Collin is a perfectionist and can be very hard on himself. He is always accountable and looks at himself first, and what he could have done better, as opposed to blaming anyone else. Since I didn't play hockey, knowing what to say and how to say it was, at times, a challenge. What I did know was that I could always listen. Sometimes, just listening was all the support he needed. Other times when we would talk, I listened, then would ask him questions to try to find the right perspective for him to relate to. One thing I want to mention is that I never sugar-coated things for him. I kept it real. There was a time in college that he was going through some adversity due to injury and we had very frank conversations. Afterward, he told me how much he appreciated me not just, "pumping his tires," like other people sometimes would.

What were the key aspects of his development that stand out to you?

Being a goalie carries a lot of pressure and I think one of the best things he did was start working with a mental performance coach shortly after high school. Mental health has gotten a lot of attention over the last 15 years and the stigma is changing. The, "Lift the Mask," program run by Justin Goldman is a great example of how people have begun to address the importance of mental health issues. Cognitive training and sports therapy have come a long way and there are more resources available now, than ever before. Since brain development continues through our early twenties, I think it's important for young people to work with brain health/development professionals, early on, to learn awareness, techniques, and strategies to handle and process stress. Perhaps, if they can learn how to move on to the next shot after a goal or move onto the next game after a loss, they may be able to enjoy the position more, perform better, ultimately having a better experience, and maybe even have a longer career.

Do you get nervous watching games and if so how do you combat those nerves?

I am a passionate person, so it's not always easy staying calm, cool, and collected especially at hockey games. It's almost as if I am fighting nature. As a goalie mom, I thought it was important to remain objective and composed, in case others were watching how I reacted. I am still cognizant of this and try to keep my emotions in check at games. No matter what, at the end of the day, it's still your kid on the ice, regardless of what age or level they play at.

What is one piece of advice you would give other goalie parents?

If I could give one piece of advice it would be to let the kids find their own passion and then help them pursue their dreams. Collin playing professionally was never a focus, rather more like a fun fantasy that a lot of little kids talk about. We just went from year to year with the idea that Collin just loved playing the game. However, as time went on, he showed signs of long-term potential and started receiving interest from scouts. More opportunities opened up and, therefore, more decisions had to be made. I think it's important if kids get to the point of being a Junior, College, or a Pro Prospect, to find out as much information as you can and get the resources necessary to help guide them. This can be quite a daunting task, but if you ask enough questions, you will at least be able to help point them in the right direction. Once again working on having that perspective throughout the journey will pay big dividends. Collin has always been the kid that the sun shines on but he's worked hard and earned every opportunity. It's nice to see that good things happen to good people and for him to be able to play at this level has been inspiring!

FAQ's

What is the difference between scouting and recruiting?

I've been very fortunate to have been a professional goaltending scout for the Toronto Maple Leafs and a college recruiter for Merrimack College, my alma mater. I can tell you with first-hand experience that being a scout and a college recruiter are two completely different things. There are challenges at both ends and they seem very similar but they are quite different.

A scout's job is to go to games and evaluate players and write reports. After the reports have been written, the scout ranks the player with respect to how much interest they have in acquiring the player. Acquiring a player for scouts is either drafting, a free agent signing, or trade. The thing about a professional is that the scout most likely will never coach a player or interact with them after the acquisition process. Once the player is acquired then the responsibility of that player falls on other people and departments. The greatest part about being a scout is that you are assessing a player's skill level and ability to help your team but do not have to convince that player to come to your program. Your team simply drafts or acquires the player.

A recruiter is typically a combination of a coach and a scout and the big difference between a recruiter and a pro scout is that not only do they have to identify the player but if they are interested they will have to convince the player to come to the program and once they get there to coach them. Therefore, a recruiter is going to have contact with the player after they come to the team and this changes the entire dynamics and the relationship between the scout and the player.

The scout simply looks for the best player available while a recruiter looks for someone that they would like to work with and spend a considerable amount of time together. When you refer to a recruiter often they are representing a school or an academy while a scout is representing either a program, junior or professional organization. At the end of the day, the scout is a buyer (acquiring an asset) while the recruiter is a seller (selling their program or school).

How do I know if my goalie is a prospect?

I remember having a conversation in my early years as a coach with a goaltender and his father. They asked me a pretty simple straightforward question of which school, Boston College or Boston University, would be the right fit. We had a really good discussion where we analyzed the pluses and minuses of both schools. It was only at the end of the conversation that I was informed that the goalie had not been recruited by either of the schools and we had just spent all this time planning and analyzing a fictitious situation.

I do get asked the same question quite often, "is my son or daughter a prospect?" After years in this business, it is now clear to me that if someone is asking me if their goalie is a prospect the answer is probably no. Nobody should have to tell a parent or a goalie if they are a prospect. They are prospects if they are getting scouted and recruited by teams. If the goalie is not being solicited by programs and schools or to play for them they are probably not a prospect. Therefore, the parents of goalies should value the interest level on where their goalie stands as opposed to someone's opinion.

I had the good fortune to be the head coach of Brooks School, a prep school in North Andover Massachusetts, for three seasons. It may have been the funnest three years that I ever experienced as a coach. We won the

Eberhart Championship all three years even making it one season to the New England Championships. I remember standing in the middle of the locker room before we went out on the ice the very first day asking the team to describe themselves. They told me how talented and hard-working they were and that they were one of the best teams in the league. That all sounded great until I asked them one simple question... What was your record last year? Well, they had missed the playoffs and finished with a losing record. From that point forward I made it a point to be very clear and regardless of the picture they wanted to paint the record was really what they were and after every game we called out our record and went on a great 3-year run.

The point of telling the Brooks story is to draw comparisons to what is real and what is perceived. A goaltender may perceive themselves as a prospect but that may not be grounded with any facts. What they should simply be focusing on is getting better and if they get good enough the interest will come. Regardless of what somebody may say such as a goalie coach, fellow team parent, or friend you may want to pay attention to the interest that your son or daughter is receiving because that is truly what is going to tell you what is real and what is perceived. I don't mean to tell you that if a goaltender is not being scouted and recruited that they do not have a chance to play at the highest levels but it does tell you where they are at that particular point in their career.

Should I be promoting my goalie?

I can't tell you how many times I've been asked this question and it actually isn't an easy answer. Parents of goalies sometimes see other goalies being scouted and recruited and wonder if they should be doing something to promote their son or daughter. There is a fear a parent has that maybe they are not doing enough that would help while other parents are doing something different.

There's a simple rule that I use called the 90/10 rule that I think all parents should be aware of. It is truly only 10% of the goalies that get all the attention while 90% of the goalies are trying to attract the attention of the scouts and recruiters. Building off the last question about whether a goalie is a prospect, it should be apparent to you if your goalie is in the 10%. When it comes to college recruiting I always say the same thing... 10% of goalies get recruited to colleges while 90% of the goalies are recruiting the colleges. If you have the chance to be in the 10% you should stay in the 10% and not worry about promoting. If you are in the 90% what your goalie can do to bring awareness to themselves and hopefully attract some interest.

When it comes to the NHL draft there are no shortages of experts trying to predict what round and what position players are going to be selected. Very few people can actually be proficient in predicting the results of the draft but ironically there is one simple method that can at least get you in the ballpark. The NHL has a combine before each draft where they invite approximately 100 of the top players in the world to be tested and interviewed. Teams have to go through the NHL front office to request interviews with the players and there is not enough time for each team to interview all 100 players. Therefore, they have to make choices with respect to which players they will talk to. The NHL receives all the requests and puts together the interview schedule of the prospects. If you take a look at how many interview requests a player receives, that is actually the best way to predict where that player is going to be drafted. Therefore, if a player receives 27 interview requests you can be pretty sure he's going to go early on in the draft. If another player receives only 7 interview requests it's a pretty good bet that he could be a late pick or no pick at all. Once again you're seeing how you don't have to ask where a player sits for the draft. All you need to know is how many interview requests they have to give you a better idea of it and where they will be selected.

Web Presence

If a goalie is in the 90%, there is a simple way, other than stopping pucks, to help with the scouting or recruiting process. Starting at the age of 14, I would suggest that goalies start their own web page. The page should consist of the following current information.

- Background and Contact Information on the Goalie.

- Academic Information.

- Schedule and Stats.

- References and References Contact Information.

- Game Video Clips.

Everything on this list is pretty self-explanatory and the video should be clips of no longer than 3 minutes and represent the best qualities a goalie has to offer. There should be no more than 6-8 seconds between saves in the video and the background should be the sounds of the rink and not music tracks. There is also no reason to put goals against in the short videos because if the coach is interested then they may request full game videos in the future. The reason why these websites are so valuable is that the goalie is in control of the content and it can be updated at any time.

There is one thing that is consistent across the board whether we're talking about academies, prep schools, junior teams, or college coaches...that is there is a finite amount of time the coaches and recruiters have to watch players, and therefore, the easier that a goalie can make their job the better off they will be. If a goaltender has their own website they can simply send a three or four-line email to the coach with a copy of the link that will take the coach to the goalie site. From the site, the coach will have all the information that they need and not be required to save or download the video onto their computer. Because the site is live, the goalie can update their site with new videos and stats at any time. Here's a good example of what an email to a coach could look like...

> Hi Coach,
>
> This is John Smith and I'm a goaltender for the XYZ team. I am interested in your program and would like to find out more about your goalie situation. Here is a link with my hockey information as well as a three-minute video. Thank you and I'm looking forward to hearing from you.
>
> John Smith

By sending a short email directly to the coach which is personalized, it should be enough to incentivize the coach to take a few minutes to click on the website. I will guarantee that the first thing that they do when they get to the site is click on the video. Make sure the video contains a lot of action and is not a highlight video with a goalie flip-flopping around with a popular techno track playing in the background. The video should consist of solid saves with a few big stops mixed in. Another key aspect to the success of sending short emails to coaches is that it comes directly from the goaltender and not the goalies' parents.

Something that you should understand when sending out emails is that once a coach receives an email like this they will immediately know the goalie is not in the 10%. This is absolutely fine if the goalie is in the 90% group and this is what they have to do to try to get more eyes on them. If a goaltender is in the 10% they should refrain from sending these emails because it will devalue them to the coaches. Personally, I've had a lot of success drawing interest in goalies because of the personal websites and I hope that this works for you and your goalie as well.

The way the personal website can be used by a parent is to explain to your son and daughter what branding is and that all athletes are actually brands. Branding is about perceived value and what a goaltender wants to do is demonstrate that their brand is one of quality. Now anytime there's a decision facing a brand they have to decide what impact that decision will have on their brand. Will that decision add value to their brand or negatively affect them? When your son or daughter is put in a situation where they have to make a decision they can simply refer to how that decision will impact their brand. Hopefully when they are faced with tough decisions that a lot of young people are faced with they will make the decision that will impact their brand most positively.

What is the difference between an agent and an advisor?

As a goaltender gets older and established, some agents and advisors can help in the scouting and recruiting process. Typically a goalie that projects as an NHL draft pick will be solicited by NHL-certified agents. The recruiting of goalies by these agents starts around the age of fourteen to fifteen. The goal of the agent is to make money when their client turns pro and therefore they are typically very particular of whom they take on as clients and only the top kids are represented by NHL agents.

In addition to NHL-certified agents, some non-certified advisors are available to work with goalies and parents to find opportunities. These advisors typically receive an annual fee from the families that they are working for. At this point, there is no certification or accreditation associated with being a hockey advisor.

As a parent, it is important when your goalie is approached to understand the difference between an NHL-certified agent and a paid advisor. When choosing an agent or advisor the process to make the best decision should be to gauge the interaction with your son or daughter, research which players they have worked with, and most importantly due your due diligence with respect to seeking out referrals and speaking to them about their experience.

How to choose a college or university?

The decision of which university to attend for families is a big one. When it comes to choosing a college or university there is a lot of time that goes into the process with both the parents and their goalie speculating about where they would best fit. For the elite goaltender, that is being recruited by NCAA Division I schools or top CIS schools, the truth of the matter is that everything happens in two weeks. The reason it revolves around two weeks is that when an actual scholarship offer gets put on the table the clock starts to click. Typically after an offer is made the agent or advisor to the elite goalie will then reach out to other potential schools and inform them of the offer. If any of the other schools are interested they will also make offers. Anything, before an offer is made, is basically the equivalent of kicking tires. It only becomes real after the first offer is made and once all the offers get put on the table a choice is made and the process is over.

For goalies that are not at the scholarship level a lot of time will be spent on visiting the schools and researching the programs. Learning about the academic tracks and the hockey program will take some time and visits are essential to finding the environment that offers the best fit. Speaking to current and former players and their parents about their experience at the schools will be invaluable. Learning about the schools' goalie situation may give you a look into the opportunity to be the starter on the team. Once again don't forget about the saying of "go where you're wanted". A goalie's best chance of ice time will likely be the coach that expresses the most interest and can lay out a potential plan.

What is the NCAA Clearinghouse?

Now Called the NCAA Eligibility Center. The NCAA Clearinghouse is an essential step in becoming eligible to play college sports. The Eligibility Center is the organization within the NCAA that determines the academic eligibility and amateur status for all NCAA DI and DII athletes. The NCAA Eligibility Center certifies whether prospective college athletes are eligible to play sports at NCAA Division I or III institutions. It does this by reviewing the student athlete's academic record, SAT® or ACT scores, and amateur status to ensure conformity with NCAA rules. The process of getting cleared by the NCAA requires steps that need to be completed by the athlete, the high school counselor, the SAT or ACT testing organization, and the university. Anyone that wants to play NCAA sports at Division I or III schools, needs to register for a Certification Account with the NCAA Eligibility Center.

How can my goalie be evaluated fairly?

When it comes to evaluations, one thing to keep in mind is that they are subjective. Whether your son or daughter is selected for a team, program or school is a representation of the opinion of the person making the decision. This has always been an area of frustration because it is not like in golf where two players play against each other and the player with the lowest score wins. That is not necessarily the case for goalies especially in a tryout situation where one goalie may give up more goals but in the opinion of the evaluator they are the better goalie. As a parent, I think it's important to explain to your son or daughter how this selection process is subjective, and therefore, a negative result does not mean the end of the line.

This is exactly the reason that I developed the SIG Game Day app. This easy-to-use, intuitive app is used in real-time to record a goaltender's performance objectively. The app tracks goal expectancy, rebound retention, glove performance, and playmaking. It was designed to be used in real-time and can instantaneously produce results of how a goalie is playing objectively. A head coach can have a conversation with the goalie coach after the game and have the key metrics from the game at the touch of a finger. Parents can have conversations with their goalies, not based on their opinion of how their goalie played in the game, but rather what the stats show. The goal of the app is to create an environment where coaches, goalie coaches, goalies, and parents can all have non-confrontational, fact-based conversations regarding a goaltender's performance.

How do I tell my goalie that they are not good enough?

As a parent, you have a role to fill and that is to support your son or daughter. There should never come a time where it is up to a parent to cut a child. I believe as a goalie coach that my role is to do everything I can to give the goaltender that I am working with the best opportunity to succeed. It is not my role to tell a goaltender that they are not good enough to play at a certain level and neither is it the responsibility of the parent to tell their goaltender that they're not good enough. We have to let our kids try and it is the responsibility of the coach to cut the goalie and not the parents. Once again a parent's job is to support and by no means should a parent be put in the situation to have to be the ones to tell their child that they're not good enough.

Should I keep my goalie off social media?

With social media so important to young people, I can't see how keeping them away from it is even going to be possible. There's so much excellent content for goalies on social media it would be a shame not to let our kids learn more about the position and the people playing the position because of some of the downsides. The one thing we have to teach our kids is that posting anything is a reflection of their brand and therefore, a negative post can reflect negatively on them.

The last thing a goalie wants to do is to criticize other goalies or teams on social media. I don't think any goalie would like to read negative remarks about them online and neither should they be commenting negatively on anybody in the goalie fraternity. We should all be supporting each other and be positive.

This also goes for the parents. More times than I would like to admit I have had to deal with issues of goalie parents making comments about their son or daughter's team, teammates, or opposition… even at the pro level! As a parent, all we want to do is help our kids but I will guarantee you that any disparaging comments on social media will tag you with a label and could impact the opportunities for your son or daughter moving forward.

What advice can I give my goalie during times of adversity?

As someone that's worked with goaltenders for the past 25 years, I think by now I've seen almost everything. There are a few sayings that I use quite frequently that maybe you can tuck in your back pocket and pull out as needed.

1. Predictable unpredictability.

One thing that I can attest to in the world of goaltending is the unpredictability of decision-making as coaches are predictable. A lot of times goalies get frustrated with the decisions of coaches, whether it is playing time or not making a team. Sometimes a goalie can over-analyze a situation and work themselves into a frenzy because it just doesn't seem logical. A lot of the decisions that are made are not necessarily logical because coaches are human and they will make the decisions based on the emotion of how they perceive a particular situation. Although something may seem as clear as day to you as a parent and a goalie, the coach may just see it another way. You have to understand that this is just the way it is and we must keep moving forward.

2. Relentless positivity.

If a goalie is going to be successful they are going to have to go through some hard times. During those hard times, it will be easy to get negative and complain. The motto of relentless positivity simply means that no matter what happens you have to dig in and stay positive because nothing can be gained by being anything other. Relentless positivity is definitely not easy. It seems easy talking about it during the good times but when those hard times come it's going to be a grind. As a parent, you can point out when times are tough and reinforce the concept of relentless positivity.

3. Being comfortable being uncomfortable.

For goalies, things will likely never be perfect. A big challenge for goalies is being comfortable being uncomfortable. If a goalie isn't comfortable it means that they are focusing on outside distractions. Picture what it would be like for an NHL goalie to travel into a city to play a game... maybe their plane was delayed because of weather and instead of arriving at midnight after playing that night they are getting in at 4 AM and have to play a game the next day. Therefore, they canceled the morning skate and the goalie that is scheduled to play has now gotten in at 4 a.m. and has no morning skate to go through the regular protocol for the game. When it comes time to drop the puck that goalie has to focus simply on stopping the puck and not get distracted by any events of the day.

4. Nobody cares.

There may be times when a goalie is in a game that they don't feel 100%. Maybe they had a tough day at school, had an argument with a friend, struggled on a quiz, or physically just don't feel like themselves. The issue for a goalie is that regardless of anything that happened during the day or what's going on in their life, no one at that rink really cares other than how they perform in the game at that time. When my son Joey played his first game in the National Hockey League he had been on a whirlwind of travel leading up to the game. The Sens were in last place and playing their third game in four nights. Joey had little sleep, a total of one team NHL practice and it was time to face the Buffalo Sabres in a sold-out arena for their last home game of the season. The time between the game and warm-up felt like it took forever as they performed both the US and Canadian national anthem and had on-ice presentations. While Joey was on the ice during the never-ending pre-game ceremonies he just kept repeating to himself...no one cares. No one cared about anything other than how he played and that mindset allowed him to push past any fatigue or nerves and go out and play a game where he was peppered with 40 shots.

5. Go where you are wanted.

Trying to decide which team, program, or school to go to is often a draining ordeal. I've been in countless situations with schools and their families trying to decide the best opportunity for their son or daughter. After years of seeing successes and failures, there is one mindset that has proved most successful in decision-making and that is... go where you're wanted. Basically when you go where you are wanted you have the best probability to play and not back up. The key to getting better is having the opportunity to play and in my experience kids that go to the program that wants them the most, usually have the most success.

6. A goalie is what you play, not who you are.

One of the most endearing qualities of a goaltender is how much they care about the position and how hard they try to give their teammates a chance to win. The one thing that they have to realize is that a goalie is just a position that they play in a game and it's not who they are. They are a son, a daughter, a grandson, a friend, a mentor, a leader, a teammate, etc. It is important to encourage your kids to be competitive and take the game seriously while at the same time not being too hard on themselves. Once in a while, it is a good reminder to let them know that they are much more than just a goalie.

What should I expect from my goalie's coach?

One of the bigger frustrations that goalie parents may have is with the actions of the head coach. Whether it is the way they communicate with the goalies, the types of drills that are run at practice, or the decision of allocating ice time, there's no shortage of bewilderment in the parents' experience. When I'm asked regarding issues parents are experiencing with their coach I routinely have to urge them to lower their expectations.

Most coaches were never goalies themselves and don't have a good understanding of what it means to be a goalie or the parent of a goalie. I have been at this a long time and for me, the easiest philosophy in dealing with coaches is to take a page out of the stoic playbook and lower your expectations. If you lower your expectations your frustration level will decrease as you just plain expect less. I wish it wasn't this way and I wish I could write something different in this section but based on my experience this is just the way it is and something goalies and their parents are just going to have to deal with. If you have a coach that is knowledgeable about the position and knows how to manage goalies be grateful and appreciative.

What can I do at home to help my goalie?

In the past, the easy answer to this question was to have your son or daughter shoot pucks in the basement, stretch, do strength and conditioning exercises, juggle and watch NHL games on TV but now it's a whole different ball game. Sense Arena, a leading company in virtual reality, has developed an app specifically for goalies that replicates the same shots and scenarios a goalie might see in a real game. Note... this is not a game! This is a training device and it also gives goaltenders analysis and feedback of their performance in the drills. In just two years the advancement of the

243

technology has been incredible and there are over thirty pro goalies currently training on Sense Arena regularly.

One of the primary reasons that virtual reality training is so good for the goalies is that it allows them to get to see plays develop and read shot releases without any wear and tear on their bodies. Equally as important is a goaltender that has virtual reality training can put on their Oculus Quest and train whenever it suits them. That means they can use the program to prepare for a practice, a game, or to give them practice whenever they choose. What makes it such a valuable tool is that it can help limit pregame anxiety and I know, as someone that had a lot of issues and was often mentally drained before a game would start, Sense Arena would have been a great tool for me to work on my mental game.

Goalie Parent Interview #11: Chris Oettinger

A native of Lakeville, Minnesota, Jake Oettinger was the first goalie selected at the 2017 NHL draft and currently plays for the Dallas Stars of the National Hockey League. Jake made the successful jump from Lakeville North High School to the US National Program and competed at both the U17 and U18 World Championships in 2015 winning a silver and gold medal respectively. He also won a silver medal at the U18 World Championships in 2016 and was a bronze medal winner at the 2018 World Junior Championships. In the NCAA, Jake excelled at Boston University and in 2018 won the Hockey East Championship while being named MVP of the tournament.

When did your son decide to be a goalie?

Jake was rotating between being a goaltender and a player as a squirt. At one point they played a tournament where Jake played all the games and they ended up winning the championship. He played very well and had a great time. He loves to win and from that point onward he just wanted to be a goalie.

What did you feel about that decision?

I had no issue with him being a goalie because I never had to ask if he wanted to go to the rink. He wanted to get on the ice as much as he could. It was really easy for us because he had a great group of friends and it was an equally great group of parents.

What has been the best part of the journey so far?

There have been so many memorable moments up to this point but the best part of the journey has been watching him do something that he loves.

It has been exciting to watch him achieve his dreams on and off the ice and he has more goals in mind.

What has been the most challenging part of being a goalie parent?

As a parent, it is always tough to watch your kid struggle. The one thing you learn as a goalie parent is how quickly the lows can turn into highs. As a goalie, there are some mental struggles and after games, I just tried to listen and let him talk through it. For me, I like to go for a walk after a tough one just to move forward and leave it behind.

What were the key aspects of his development that stand out to you?

One of the things we did not do is a lot of jumping around from team to team. Jake stayed in the same organization and was able to move up to the top team at each level. The levels had two birth years so he was able to play with older kids every other year. The key was he was given the opportunity to play and as the only goalie saw a lot of game action.

Do you get nervous watching games and if so how do you combat those nerves?

I find that I do get anxious before games. I do not eat a lot and it is really the lead-in that brings it on. Once the game starts and I see where it is going I am fine. I prefer to sit down at Jake's end so I can see him better and will move from end to end after each period if possible. During Covid, we watched games almost every other night in the family room and it was great spending that time as a family.

What is one piece of advice you would give other goalie parents?

My advice to another goalie parent is pretty simple...be patient. There are so many paths that a goalie can take and there is no one clear-cut way. Jake started as a JV goalie and as opposed to being frustrated he just worked hard and kept earning opportunities. A goalie just has to stay at it and eventually they will get their opportunity. Once they get their chance it is up to them.

Conclusion

This book starts with a picture on the cover of my son Joey when he won his first game in the NHL. The symbolism of the celebratory fist pump with the stairs in the background after a challenging game captures the journey of a goaltender. The game had just about everything in it from the originally scheduled starter Matt Murray leaving the ice in warm-up, Joey getting run over on the very first play of the game, some missed empty nets by the Senators to lock the game down, and even a dramatic late surge by the Maple Leafs. It all made for an exciting finish, a moment we will never forget as a family.

The game wasn't that far off the roller coaster of a journey that ended up with a kid living out his dream and a couple of parents and a younger brother being along for the ride. It's amazing to think back about all the ups and downs, the long talks, all the hard decisions along the way that led to getting to that point. The one consistent theme that I was able to get from the goalie parent interviews for this book was to make sure to enjoy the ride. There was such a recurring message of being patient and staying in the present...it was undeniable. The parents as a whole had such a great appreciation for the journey as opposed to the outcome and it was inspiring to me as a goalie parent. They were grateful for the friendships along the way, the travel and tournaments, and watching their kids learn valuable lessons as they mature into adults. There are easier paths than choosing to be a goalie but I don't know of too many positions in sports that will better prepare a young man or woman for the rigors of life.

I can't thank you, the reader, enough for taking the time to read this book. I hope that what I was able to share in these pages will help you and your goalie so that they can maximize their enjoyment for the game of hockey and being a goaltender. Take it from a veteran goalie parent that the time will go by quickly and you will long to return to the early morning practices, the long road trips, and most importantly the time you spend with your kids.

About the Author

Brian Daccord is a worldwide leader and innovator in goaltending development. He has served as Goaltending Coach of the Boston Bruins, Goaltending Scout for the Toronto Maple Leafs, and the Director of Goaltending Development for the Arizona Coyotes. His coaching resume includes a six-year stint with Adler Mannheim in the German DEL and he has coached in the NCAA for Merrimack College and St Anselm College. Currently, the goaltending coach at Boston University, Brian played professionally for seven seasons in the Swiss NLA and his book "Hockey Goaltending" sold over 40,000 copies and he holds a Master's Degree in Sports Science.

Originally from the town of Beaconsfield, Quebec, Canada, Brian began playing goalie after his older brother Tom grew weary of the cold while playing on the local outdoor rinks. Inspired by the iconic mask of legendary Boston Bruins goaltender Gerry Cheevers, he began his journey as a goaltender. Experiencing hockey on the backyard rink with his father serving as his goalie coach and his older brother whipping pucks in his direction, his passion for the sport of hockey continued to grow. After several years of playing for his hometown Beaconsfield Braves, Brian played for Loyola High School winning a Provincial Championship as a Bantam.

Following High School, he played one year of junior for the West Island Royals where he was awarded a scholarship to attend Merrimack College located 25 miles outside of Boston, Massachusetts. His freshman year for the Warriors was the school's last season competing in Division II ranks before stepping into Division I and Brian started 29 of 31 games, leading his team to the national championship game eventually losing to Bemidji State.

Following his junior year of college, he signed his first professional contract with Ambri-Piotta of the Swiss National A Hockey League where he played six seasons. Suffering a knee injury that kept him out of the lineup his seventh year in Switzerland and then playing for Fribourg Gotteron, Brian retired as a player to pursue a career as a coach.

Brian Daccord's coaching career began at his alma mater Merrimack College where he served as assistant/goaltending coach for two seasons and spent one season with St Anselm College as goaltending coach, winning the Division II ECAC Championship during the 1999-2000 season. While at St Anselm College, Brian began building his private development company and 22 years later Stop It Goaltending is one of the most respected goalie schools in the world training over 1,000 goalies annually across Massachusetts.

Along with being a coach and leader in goaltending development, Brian is also the author of "Hockey Goaltending" and has appeared as a guest on top hockey podcasts as well as a keynote speaker at hockey symposiums both live and virtually. He created the goaltending scouting app called SIG Game Day, which allows goaltenders to be evaluated free of bias and subjectivity. Brian is also an advisor to Sense Arena, the leader in virtual reality training, and has assisted in developing their goaltending specific curriculum.

Brian lives in North Andover, MA with his wife Daniela and sons Joey and Alex. Joey is currently under contract with the Seattle Kraken of the NHL and Alex is a senior varsity goaltender at St. Anselm College, Manchester NH.

Made in the USA
Las Vegas, NV
14 September 2021